'No other publication that I know of hą
from the teachers'

**Professor Richard Pring, Honorary Re
College, Oʒ**

'Jon Berry shows how governments have tried to regulate and suppress
the energies that teachers can bring to classrooms – and how teachers
continue, amid constant pressure, to work by different rules. Combining
realism and optimism, accuracy and humour, his book will persuade
many readers that alternatives exist, here and now, to the grim visions of
education that dominate policy.'

**Ken Jones, Senior Policy Officer, Curriculum and Assessment, National
Union of Teachers**

'This is an important and timely book. It confirms that, despite all the
testing, setting, sorting and ranking that are the hallmark of the English
school system, teachers remain fundamentally unaltered by the panoply of
market-driven "reforms". Rather, teachers continue to be driven by a much
more optimistic and hopeful vision of education. This book reminds us
that everyday there are teachers in classrooms working hard to challenge
the dead weight of standardization and targets. More importantly, it serves
to remind us that when individual teachers organize collectively they not
only have the power to challenge the neoliberal restructuring of schools,
but also to create something much more exciting – an education that
doesn't just reproduce, but transforms.'

**Professor Howard Stevenson, Director of Research, School of Education,
University of Nottingham**

'Books like this bring hope in troubled times. Here you will read the stories
of teachers who are determined to educate and free young minds. This book
will help get teachers' voices heard above the managerial din. Jon Berry's
clear thinking cuts through the thicket of accountability and control.'

**Terry Wrigley, Visiting Professor of Education and Lifelong Learning,
Northumbria University**

'This is a well-argued and much-needed defence of teacher professionalism, at a time when a bureaucratic, punitive and often damaging accountability system seems to be undermining it at every turn. Jon Berry's is ultimately an optimistic account of how teachers can and are resisting such pressures, focusing instead on the core aspect of their job: teaching children well.'

Warwick Mansell, education journalist, former curriculum and testing correspondent, *Times Educational Supplement*

Teachers Undefeated

Teachers Undefeated

How global education reform has
failed to crush the spirit of educators

Jon Berry

Foreword by Christine Blower

  is an imprint of

First published in 2016 by the UCL Institute of Education Press, 20 Bedford Way, London WC1H 0AL

www.ucl-ioe-press.com

British Library Cataloguing in Publication Data:
A catalogue record for this publication is available from the British Library

ISBNs
978-1-85856-678-8 (paperback)
978-1-85856-775-4 (PDF eBook)
978-1-85856-776-1 (ePub eBook)
978-1-85856-777-8 (Kindle eBook)

Typeset by Quadrant Infotech (India) Pvt Ltd
Printed by CPI Group (UK) Ltd, Croydon, CR0 4YY

Contents

Acknowledgements

My thanks go to all of you who have so willingly given time to contribute to this book. Thanks, too, for your constant confirmation that the idea behind it is an important one and that it's a theme close to your hearts. I hope that I've captured your thoughts, ideas and, of course, your commitment to better education in the way you would have wanted. To all the activists, campaigners and resisters out there who keep the sparks alive, just keep at it. *La lutte continue.*

Foreword

The NUT is delighted to recommend this book to teachers. Jon Berry has shown that despite being scrutinized, measured and assessed for the last twenty years on everything they do, teachers still hold true to a vision of teaching and learning that goes way beyond the strictures imposed by successive governments. The testimony and anecdotes from teachers that make up much of this book bear witness to hard-working, committed, thoughtful and creative practitioners. Instead of doubting them at every turn, politicians should be praising their efforts to the skies.

Jon shows how the political and economic context in which teachers work has a profound bearing on their daily professional lives. Thanks to his analysis of this context, along with some historical background, teachers new to the profession will be able to make greater sense of the wave of demands that continues to come their way. At a time when the study of pedagogy, child development and the history of education are being squeezed out of teachers' initial training, the book provides discussion of these issues, as well as a gateway to further reading on these topics.

Although it presents a clear analysis of where we are and how we got here, *Teachers Undefeated* moves towards a conclusion that talks about ways in which teachers can collectively begin to resist the effects of the GERM – the global education reform movement. The teachers whose words we hear in this book reject the GERM's meagre and measly view of education. But without this possibility of collective resistance, even the best analysis is only an academic exercise. As a campaigning, active union we always look to the way in which our actions can improve what we are able to do for the young people we work with every day.

I absolutely commend this book to you. I hope you will read and enjoy it and find time to discuss it with friends and colleagues. I believe that you will be inspired to continue to campaign for education as a human and civil right and a public good. This is at the heart of what the National Union of Teachers believes. Our children and our teachers deserve no less.

Christine Blower
General Secretary, National Union of Teachers

About the author

Dr Jon Berry is the programme director for the Professional Doctorate in Education (EdD) at the University of Hertfordshire. He taught English in comprehensive schools for 28 years before moving to the higher education sector in 2004 as a teacher educator. Since then he has pursued his research interest into teachers' professional autonomy, placing the role of the teacher against the background of the ideological drive towards marketization. His research demonstrates that despite policy overload, which leaves many teachers angry, tired and bewildered at the actions of successive governments, they still cling to a strong notion of education that genuinely puts the child at the centre. He has been an active campaigner in two education unions, the NUT and the UCU, and has been a senior lay officer in both organizations.

Introduction

From the World Bank to a classroom near you: what this book sets out to do

Most teachers love their job. That may sound like a bold statement, but after nearly forty years as a classroom teacher, activist and teacher educator, I know this to be true. Conversely, most teachers think they spend far too much time and effort on tasks and duties that sap their energy and contribute little to the learning of their students. Teachers don't mind working hard and they expect to do so: what they find dispiriting is the whole paraphernalia of the last twenty years or so, which has so complicated the straightforward – if challenging – business of getting young people interested and learning.

This book sets out to strengthen the voice of the vast majority of teachers who still hold to the belief that education is about the whole child and who believe in creating opportunities for making learning creative and exciting. They do this despite the mass of measures they encounter daily in the form of high-stakes observations, performance-related targets, the drive for results and constant, ill-considered innovations. The book challenges the notion that all of these measures, relentless and draining as teachers find them, have created a generation of educators which has bought into a narrow and reductive view of what education is for.

What follows places the experience of teachers in a political and economic context. It argues that a global, neoliberal approach to education has its impact on the daily lives of teachers and concludes by arguing that it is necessary for teachers to understand this in order to challenge it. When writing about World Bank financing of education, Jones (2007: xvii) suggests that notwithstanding 'the impact of globalization on educational theory, policy and practice … since 1990, the impact on classroom practice has not been as great as we might imagine'. This book takes issue with such analysis on two counts. First, the impact of global reform plays out most days in almost every classroom as teachers are compelled to turn their actions into measurable data. Second, it argues that *only* by placing the daily experience of the classroom teacher in this wider context can we begin to make sense of where we are as educators.

My hope is that this book will be read by teachers and that it will reinforce their belief in what they are doing. At conferences, events and in everyday conversations, it is plain that many teachers welcome such reaffirmations, faced as they are with demands that undermine their vision of what teaching could be like. Teacher educators and beginning teachers in schools and universities may also find it a useful analysis and a helpful reminder of what should be going on beyond the quest to produce proof, evidence and paperwork. I also hope that parents, school governors and anyone involved in teaching, learning and the welfare of young people will find material of interest here. By the end of the book one message should be clear – we have many thousands of inventive, committed and energetic teachers out there. What they need – and what our children deserve – is for them to be left to their own devices much more than they are at present. They are very good at what they do. Above all, whoever reads this will, I hope, choose to challenge and present alternatives whenever the opportunity arises.

Because I do want this book to be read by as wide an audience as possible (as every author does!) this is not an academic volume in the traditional sense. There are plentiful illustrative anecdotes from teachers, and the occasional minor digression. I have shamelessly used what I hope are illuminating and entertaining episodes from my own experience to reinforce some of the thinking about what is under discussion. There are, however, plentiful references to literature and sources which I hope will be used as helpful gateways for those who want to investigate further some of the issues raised here. I encourage teachers, especially those at the start of their careers, to do so.

One final note. This book relates to the situation in England and although the circumstances are contextualized as part of what is happening globally, the instances cited and references to policy and practice are specifically English. Nonetheless, teachers from many parts of the world will be familiar with what is written and will be able to associate with it.

Chapter 1

The GERM: What it is and where it comes from

One of the challenges of writing about numerous changes that have beset education in the last quarter of a century has been to find a convenient term with which to summarize the situation. In this I am grateful to Finnish writer and commentator Pasi Sahlberg for bringing the term GERM into common currency (see *pasisahlberg.com* inter alia). The term, carefully chosen for its connotations of ill health, is an acronym for the Global Education Reform Movement, and Sahlberg identifies five separate features that contribute to it. Given that the term will be used hereafter in this publication, it is worth outlining what these are. In doing so, I clearly acknowledge that these ideas form the basis of one of Sahlberg's principal publications – *Finnish Lessons* (Sahlberg, 2012). A more detailed discussion about the impact of each of these strands will inform much of what follows, so for the moment these are outlined in the broadest possible terms – but all of them will be familiar to anyone involved in education.

The first feature is *standardization of education*. From the late 1980s the drive towards outcomes-based education took hold in England and elsewhere; an analysis of how this happened is supplied in Chapter 2. While it would be absurd to argue that any attempt to drive up standards could be bad, the apparatus used to control and quantify this became a cart that drove a horse. High-stakes testing, the open publication of results in the form of league tables, punitive inspection regimes and a culture of target-setting gradually became the norm in English schools. As policy makers and schools looked for safe and reliable ways of meeting such targets, this culture led to a homogenization of policy and practice as all involved sought to ensure that bases were covered and targets met.

Stringent testing regimes and the need for measurable outcomes led to a strong focus on the second feature – a *focus on core subjects*. Primary school teachers in England, as well as many of their colleagues in secondary school, will have noted with disappointment how in the last two decades a clear hierarchy of subjects has emerged and become firmly entrenched. Along with this goes the third strand of the search for *low-risk ways to reach learning goals*. There is an inevitability about teachers seeking the best and quickest ways of generating the sort of results that any given testing regime requires at any given moment. This was captured perfectly in a recent conversation I had with a former teaching colleague, who bemoaned the fact that she once prided herself on being a very good English teacher but now thought of herself as a very good GCSE teacher.

Teachers in England will all recognize the fourth strand: *the use of corporate management models* as a means of bringing about school improvement. The borrowing – often in a clumsy and half-understood way – of the language and practices of the business world and then the shoehorning of these into the world of schools is one of the principal features of the GERM. With the increased movement toward schools becoming self-governing entities, mainly through the academies programme, the language of target-setting, performance and productivity now informs the conduct of many school leaders and their senior teams.

The final feature is the prevalence of *test-based accountability policies* for schools. As a lay official of the National Union of Teachers (NUT) I came across my first case of a teacher overtly cheating in a public examination in 2001. A teacher had opened a Key Stage 3 mathematics SATs paper two days early and had the children practise what was on it. At the time the case was outlandish, but as I write this, a simple internet search using *teacher exam cheat uk* yields results in the tens of thousands. Given the ramifications for individuals and institutions of poor results on standardized testing, such disheartening outcomes are not entirely surprising.

It is important, however, to understand that the GERM is a manifestation of wider forces. We live in times when an economic model in which neoliberalism and marketization hold sway is globally dominant. This is not an economics textbook and I am only too aware that the term 'neoliberalism' is bandied about in a way that seems to imply universal comprehension: conversations with students at all levels indicate that this is not the case. For convenience, I will borrow economist David Harvey's definition of the roots of neoliberalism lying in 'the assumption that individual freedoms are guaranteed by freedom of the market and of trade' and that this assumption is 'a cardinal feature of such thinking' (Harvey, 2005: 7). The state should limit intervention in economic matters only in emergency or in matters of national security. The prevalence, or hegemony, of such thinking provides the seedbed for educational policies which, along with all social and societal arrangements, allows what was once unconscionable to become the norm. The privatization of schooling with corporations owning chains of schools as they once might have owned garages or carpet shops is now part of the educational arrangement in England. A major educational publishing company talks in the language of 'emerging markets for faster growth, larger market opportunities and greater impact on learning outcomes' (Pearson, 2013). When such political and economic conditions prevail, it is no surprise that the GERM can flourish.

My reasons for writing this book are – in no particular order of importance – personal, political and professional. After nearly thirty years of teaching in comprehensive schools I moved into Higher Education in 2004 to become a teacher educator. I still stubbornly use this term instead of 'trainer'. After such a lengthy period of teaching adolescents in all their good, bad and ugliness it was a pleasant change to work with students who, unlike their unpredictable teenage counterparts, were reliably cheerful, optimistic, energetic and driven by a sense of purpose. Increasingly, however, I became uncomfortable about what happened to them once they went out on school placements. Inevitably, some of the shiny enthusiasm wore off as they became tired and the realities of school life struck home. It was not this that concerned me: such a reaction was to be expected. The cause of my anxiety is captured in the following story.

I find myself sitting in the back of a classroom in a comprehensive school in a leafy suburb. It is a warm and pleasant afternoon and the children in a Year 10 set seem amiable and well disposed. I know my trainee (for that is what I must call her) to be competent, well organized and thorough in everything she does. I hope I have done everything possible to put her at her ease in what I know to be a demanding situation for her. She tells me she is going to introduce the class to J.B. Priestley's play *An Inspector Calls*. I am looking forward to it.

It is worth having a word about this particular text. As a teacher it has been a perennial favourite of my own, not least because of the predictability of its impact on young people. The play ingeniously and intriguingly exposes the callous cruelty of a smug, self-satisfied and prosperous family towards a young factory worker (even as I explain this here, I am reluctant to spoil the plot for any reader who does not know the play). It is a compelling metaphor for mankind's enduring selfishness and stupidity. Having taught it over the years, I began to pride myself in measuring out just how much could be covered in individual lessons in order to finish at a suspenseful moment, leaving room for speculation about how the plot would develop. As more technology became available to me in the classroom, I was able to take advantage of a number of excellent TV and film adaptations.

The lesson begins. We are told we are studying a play. Inevitably, a murmur goes round the room expressing a desire to take a part or not – along with the inevitable enquiry as to whether we 'will be watching a video,

Miss?' But wait. Before we begin the play we are ... going to look at some historical context? No. Acquire some biographical detail about Priestley, perhaps? Not this time. Point out that there is currently a new production in the West End where audiences are still riveted by this brilliantly constructed dramatic artifice – further proof of the durability of this 50-year-old piece of work? Not on this occasion.

What we *are* going to do is to remind ourselves of the assessment criteria for the assignment we will have to complete at the end of this series of lessons. And then we are given that assignment, which my experienced eye immediately recognizes has a title that, in itself, gives away a major part of the plot. The class is then asked whether or not that title gives them some indication as to what the play may be about. I slump – although I hope not visibly. I am bound to ask myself why, after some thirty minutes of the lesson, we haven't resorted to the apparently outdated measure of reading the text or watching a film clip to find out.

The trainee performs competently. She has a pleasant but firm manner, is well prepared and her copious paperwork is in impeccable order. By way of a footnote, I am pleased to report that she is currently building a successful teaching career for herself. At the end of the lesson, when I am to feed back to her, she is accompanied by the teacher in the school assigned to be her mentor. Although my trainee has demonstrated undoubted competence, I do wish to make the point that I feel that she has not done justice to the wonderful material that Priestley has provided her. I clumsily attempt to make light of this by saying that in the unlikely event of her ever asking me to the theatre for the evening I would be forced to decline on the grounds that she'd give away the ending before we go in. The two young women look bemused. When, in more serious vein I try to point out that she should try to capture the attention and imagination of children – most of whom will be far less amenable than this likeable group – before dampening everything by talking of assessment, her mentor visibly bridles at these remarks from some daft old relic who has been let out for the afternoon from his ivory tower. The scheme of work for this play, she tells me with some spirit, has yielded very good examination grades. I hesitate over whether I should comment on such a justification, but settle for the path of least resistance and acknowledge that this is, indeed, an important consideration. I forbear to mention my strong suspicion that these children would get good grades anyway and could possibly have a good deal more fun on the way to doing so.

This is not an isolated episode. I could choose from a raft of examples. As a tutor and an experienced teacher I had attempted to encourage innovation – even daring – in my approach to my trainees and how they developed as teachers. Many were intellectually sharp, practically all were thoughtful, some were hugely funny and inventive and almost all brought a sense of deep-seated commitment to their work, along with a love of their subject. Gradually, however, as they spent more time in schools, they appeared to slip into a dull conformity and, above all, an acceptance of the need to comply with schemes and approaches that were deemed 'effective'.

My concern prompted me into a doctoral study looking at teachers' professional autonomy and their own view of this autonomy. Over some three years I interviewed teachers, gathered written testimony from them and, on many occasions, received unsolicited commentaries – often in the form of email rants – as new thoughts and ideas occurred to them or as a new government initiative was announced on the six o'clock news. The final study produced a number of findings, but the most compelling was this: for all that they felt beleaguered by the need to produce results, perform well in observations and produce reams of largely meaningless data, what Ball (2003) calls the 'soul the teacher' had not been entirely captured. The vast majority of respondents expressed clearly that they could give much more and could do so in a much more creative and interesting way – if only they were given the time, space and, as they saw it, the trust to do so.

This book draws on the testimony of those teachers. It is also based on the contributions gathered from other teachers in the twelve months up to publication. It is instructive to mention something of the way in which both sets of evidence have been collected. The most noticeable – and most gratifying – aspect of this has been the willingness with which teachers have given time and energy to their responses. Some of this could be attributed to personal loyalty: some, but by no means all, respondents were friends, former colleagues and students past and present. This alone, however, does not account for the enthusiasm with which written and spoken testimony was given, often in great volume and, to reiterate the point, often unprompted. The teachers' views about their own professional autonomy is of central concern to them and they vehemently wanted their voices heard. I am grateful to them and I hope that readers of this book will find their own thoughts and ideas resonating here as well.

I begin by providing some historical and theoretical background to the situation in which England's teachers find themselves. I hope this will be useful and interesting, especially for beginning teachers who often find themselves on courses and training programmes from which this sort of perspective has long since been removed. There follows a rather gloomy, but important, section that reveals how the GERM manifests itself in the way schools are run: if we are to resist it, we need to understand the damage it does. From there we concentrate on the energy, knowledge and determination of teachers. We hear the voices of those resolutely holding on to a better version of teaching than that which might be foisted upon them. Finally, and crucially, I consider how teachers, their representative organizations and wider coalitions can challenge current hegemony and work towards a vision of education that improves the thin and meagre provision offered by the GERM.

Chapter 2

The state we're in and how we got here: How the GERM took hold

This chapter traces some of the historical and political developments that have led us to where we are. However, one point needs to be made from the outset: there never was a golden age of teaching and education and the tone of what follows is devoid of false nostalgia. Neither is this a full history of education in England; others have already made a compelling job of doing this (Chitty, 2009; Gillard, 2011). What follows is an outline of developments in the last 40 years or so: the sources and citations that are included can also lead interested parties on a revealing treasure hunt of the rich history and commentary that exists about this era. What is important about this background is for us to consider how conditions were established that enabled the GERM to take hold.

I take as a starting point an event in October, 1976. The Prime Minister at the time was Labour's James Callaghan and he chose the occasion of the delivery of a speech at Ruskin College to venture into the world of schools and education. To a modern audience, such an event seems wholly unremarkable, but Callaghan was fully aware of the fact that he was encroaching on territory regarded at the time as beyond the remit of politicians. *The Guardian* newspaper reinforced this when it warned him that 'no principle has been more hallowed by British governments than the rule that they should not interfere in the curriculum of state schools'. Nonetheless, Callaghan adopted a new register and language as far as education was concerned, identifying the need for schools and teachers to 'examine … priorities and to secure as high efficiency as possible by the skilful use of existing resources' (Callaghan, 1976). In other words, money was running out and good results – the 'high efficiency' of which he speaks – needed to be guaranteed.

Callaghan recognized that by stepping into what he dubbed 'the secret garden' of schools and education he would be breaking with precedent. His need to do so, which I discuss below, was eased a little by the case of William Tyndale school in North London, which was used as proof positive by a gleeful media that 'modern methods' were some kind of woolly-minded left-wing experiment to be foisted on working-class children by feckless, politically motivated teachers. That the truth was somewhat different was immaterial (see Gretton and Jackson, 1976). Callaghan's speech had opened up schools, teachers and education in general to a discourse of value for money, employability and accountability that most commentators agree marks the beginning of the current age.

Callaghan was reacting to political and economic circumstance. Some twenty years earlier, his Conservative predecessor, Harold Macmillan, was able to opine that most of the people of Britain had never had never had it so good and, broadly speaking, in the wake of post-war austerity and in an age of full employment resulting in the acquisition by working-class families of a range of formerly unobtainable consumer goods, this was not an outlandish claim. By the time Callaghan assumed office, however, such economic optimism was a thing of the past and all public services found themselves affected by this downturn in events. Notions of value for money, along with an emerging discourse of falling standards, opened the way for a period of reform and scrutiny of education, eventually culminating in the Education Reform Act (ERA) of Margaret Thatcher's government in 1988 and, from there, to the introduction of the National Curriculum and all of its attendant measures.

Thatcher came to office in 1979, some nine years before the introduction of ERA, but the ideological grounds for intervention into this area of public service had been carefully laid. In a clear signal of what lay ahead, one of her government's first actions was to honour an election pledge to allow the purchase of council housing, thereby appropriating to the private domain that which previously had been publicly owned. As a pointer about what was to come, nothing could have been clearer. Public services were all up for sale. In the years up to the introduction of ERA, the policy discourse of the time was dominated by the idea that social institutions were in a state of crisis and that any fiscal intervention at state level was entirely contingent upon value for money (Ball, 2008). Along with this, an orchestrated attack on trade unions – most spectacularly in the miners' strike of 1984–5 – and a willingness to quash dissent by means of an evermore militarized police force, helped reinforce the idea that there was an increasingly strong and irresistible power lodged within the state (Gamble, 1988). Thatcher's famous dictum that 'there is no such thing as society', just individual men and women, has become a telling epigram for an age in which neoliberalism took hold and the prevalence of the market imposed itself on all areas of public life.

For teachers, the most immediate effect of the ERA was the introduction of the National Curriculum. For those interested in the machinations behind its content and the part played by leading individuals, the account given by one of the chief participants, Brian Cox, makes compelling reading (Cox, 1995). Teachers at the time, however – and I was Head of English, the most highly-contested curriculum area – soon settled into the task of adjusting what they already did to fit the demands of this newly itemized world. The real horrors of standardized tests, published league tables and punitive inspections – the means of controlling teachers' actions and measuring output – were still a few years away. These later measures, through which the Office for Standards in Education (Ofsted) became so central to the professional lives of teachers nearly thirty years on, emerged from the centralization inherent in the introduction of the National Curriculum. Importantly, these mechanisms arose from the need to check on its delivery – a term unheard of in educational circles before that time, which, although greeted with hilarity and disbelief, has now become entirely normalized. It is not difficult to see how this set of circumstances created fertile ground for the breeding of the GERM, as these ideas took hold not just in England but in other parts of the globe as well.

This broader idea of 'effectiveness' was firmly established in schools and colleges of education in England by the time of the ERA. As early as 1981, Brian Simon had written his seminal essay about the way in which the training of teachers in England was somehow taking place without the inclusion of any serious discussion of pedagogy (Simon, 1981). Some 23 years later, his colleague Robin Alexander detected no improvement in this situation (Alexander, 2004). By 2011, a government document outlining how to train 'the next generation of outstanding teachers' failed to use the term 'pedagogy' in its entire text (Department for Education (DfE), 2011). This stripping out of any broader considerations of the nature and purpose of education by those charged with its 'delivery' is instructive and a reflection of the pursuit of 'raising standards' above all else. The importance of this argument merits further discussion.

It is worth starting by reiterating the point made in the first chapter: teachers want to raise standards. The claims by various secretaries of state for education, culminating in Michael Gove's infamous suggestion that those who had the temerity to question his dubious innovations were the enemies of promise, are unwarranted slurs (Gove, 2013). Many teachers enter the profession with clear notions of making a contribution to society or even redressing social injustices. For some, education is seen as an emancipatory project, sitting within a strong notion of liberal humanism (Harris, 2007).

Others are driven by a love of subject or even a love of learning per se. The notion that anyone would embark on such a demanding and exhausting occupation with the intent of stifling progress is clearly risible. As the testimony from teachers in this book will demonstrate, most cling fiercely to a concept of education as a liberal humanist project – though they may not articulate it in such terms – with the child at the centre. In a neoliberal world, however, education is seen primarily as the producer of human capital. There is nothing particularly new or unique about this. Writing about the first of the great education acts, Fortser's Act of 1870, historian George Cole suggests that such provision was made by the state very much in order to meet its own needs:

> Industry needed operatives who were able to read its rules and regulations, and an increasing supply of skilled workers able to work to drawings and to write at any rate a simple sentence. The State needed more civil servants and local government employees for the developing tasks of public administration. The growing professions needed more skilled helpers. And, apart from all of this ... the new world of machine production and parliamentary government made illiteracy more and more a nuisance which had to be put down.
>
> (Cole and Postgate, 1938: 356–7)

The tension between the conception of education as a humanistic project or one for the production of human capital is, therefore, an historical and enduring one. To return to the earlier point about false nostalgia for a non-existent golden age, there has never been a time when the state was not interested in what the education system produced. The prosperous 1950s Britain of Macmillan's claims would have seemed even more promising for that 20 per cent of the population identified by the 11-plus examination and earmarked for free university education and the expanding number of white-collar professions. For schools at that time, the extent of their obligation to the state was to produce this quota, needed to meet the requirements of the expanding professional class or else equipping those with sufficient skill to service manufacturing and industry. In a world still requiring a reservoir of unskilled labour, education as the producer of human capital was comfortably able to fulfil this function. Against such a background, space existed for teachers to act in a more autonomous and individualistic way – not *always* to the benefit of young people – that seems unthinkable to their modern counterparts. Dale (1989) captures what this meant for teachers in his formulation of the move from a licensed autonomy to a regulated one.

In a world where schools and the education system were broadly doing what the state required them to do, the need for what we might now call the micro-management of schools and teachers was not pressing. The following anecdote serves to illustrate this more fully.

Like many young people, one of the reasons I chose to enter teaching was because of the example of an inspirational teacher. As a teenager preparing for my O level year (the predecessor of GCSE) I found myself in the class of an outlandish, bohemian English teacher who introduced us to books, discussions and ideas that were beyond the experience of any of us in the class – and we loved every peculiar, unpredictable minute of it. One morning in early April, some six weeks before the examination itself, a friend cautiously asked what we needed to do to revise. Somewhat grudgingly, we were presented with a few past papers, furnished with some regulation tricks-of-the-trade in terms of passing exams and, some three months later, duly came out with the good grades we required. We had been educated first and prepared for the test second. It was a model I used unrelentingly in my own teaching career and it served young people well – and produced the grades and outcomes to keep the emergent class of number-crunchers in my school's management team content. As the testimony that follows in later chapters reveals, it is the model that most teachers would like to adopt. What I experienced in my English class fits perfectly with Dale's notion of a licensed autonomy; for most teachers, however, it is regulation – and heavy-handed regulation at that – which more closely characterizes their current working environment.

It is important to analyse this apparent need for regulation and the almost constant scrutiny of teachers' practice which is its by-product. In order to do this, it is useful to introduce the term 'performativity'. Ball (2008: 49) defines performativity as 'a culture or a system of terror' that has a daily impact upon the way in which teachers feel themselves controlled and, simultaneously, impelled to buy into a system of productivity that is used to measure the value of both their individual worth and that of their institution. If teachers are to be managed – if they are to perform – in a culture of outcomes, outputs and scrutiny, this can only make sense if identifiable indicators are available. At its worst, this casts children as units of production and schools as the business-like organizations that generate such products. The indicators and outputs used are, primarily, test results, and along with these go a larger apparatus including the open publication of inspection reports, attendance figures and the collection of a plethora of questionable data that keeps a managerial class occupied and continually nervous – a nervousness that is imparted to teachers on a daily basis. All of this stems from a political and ideological imperative that sees the market as a driving force.

The need for measurable outcomes as a means of assessing productivity is illustrated by the importance that has been attached by politicians to the Programme for International Student Assessment (PISA) established through the Organisation for Economic Co-operation and Development (OECD) in 1997. These figures are often used by politicians in a somewhat cavalier way depending on where individual countries finish in any set of league tables for a particular period. However, their very existence points to a system that now sees comparison, competition and measurability as essential parts of how it functions, even though such comparison is not part of PISA or the OECD's intention, and the understanding of this by politicians of all hues seems a touch imperfect (Morris and Nash, 2013). The hijacking of a system indicating educational achievement, however imperfect such a system may be, for use as a means of generating dubious international comparison for political capital, is a further instance of the marketization of education.

What all this leads to is a need to 'produce', as if young people were cans of beans and not individual human beings. When we add to this the fact that institutional success and the job security of teachers are dependent on such production, along with their very working conditions, it might be unsurprising if they took the path of least resistance and looked for the quickest, proven ways of producing the results they need. Alexander (2004) characterizes this entirely understandable approach as an espousal of the 'what works' agenda. On the face of it, such an approach makes perfect sense, but as we will hear from practitioners, when this becomes the overriding culture in schools, what can follow is a thin, reductive and somewhat joyless approach to teaching and learning. It is worth restating one of the central arguments of this book: teachers are duty-bound to work with their students to get the best results and outcomes for them that they possibly can. It does not follow, however, that the way to achieve such results is through a regime of rehearsal, constant testing, the checking and re-checking of data and the need to be constantly observed and graded as a professional.

This apparent need for constant checking has led to the emergence of a new hero of the hour: the middle manager. On a personal note, the extent of my professional ambition as a schoolteacher was to be a Head of English – something I accomplished and then carried out for nearly twenty years. I had hoped I had achieved this through a thorough knowledge of my beloved subject, a willingness to learn and experiment professionally and through an application of a modest understanding of pedagogy. When the notion that I was a middle manager crept into the lexicon of meetings and conversations, I was never quite sure whether to take umbrage or merely giggle at such silliness. Now, as a teacher educator, I regularly meet former students who proudly, and properly, tell me of their latest rapid promotion to 'managerial' posts. Saddled as they are with student debt and performance-related pay, it would be churlish of me to begrudge them such success. It is, however, a clear reflection of how neoliberal approaches have made an impact on the way in which schools organize themselves and how some teachers perceive notions of success. All of this fits with the pervasive notion of 'production': if our job is to produce, then it follows that this production needs to be carefully managed.

This managerial model of how schools operate is underpinned in England by the current advocacy of academies and free schools. Governments of various persuasions in England since 1988 have been either complicit in, or energetic backers of, the dismantling of democratically elected local bodies who organize school provision, placing responsibility for the education of young people into the hands of private providers (Benn, 2011; Chitty, 2009; see also *antiacademies.org.uk*). The pathway to this overt privatization of education was opened up by the ERA in 1988. Although the introduction of the National Curriculum was, for teachers, the most immediate and obvious effect of the Act, it was the simultaneous provision for schools to become independent financial entities through the introduction of Local Management of Schools (LMS) that was to have just as lasting an effect. The humble school bursar was replaced by specialist financial assistance and the role of the headteacher began to move inexorably to the contemporary model of the Chief Executive as the balance sheet took precedence over the daily rough-and-tumble of school life. The Act also made provision for open enrolment of students, thereby undermining the role of local bodies in planning and organizing admissions, as well as putting into place the first mechanisms for publicly funded schools to opt out of Local Authority control – the clear forerunner of the academies and free schools project.

Importantly, the introduction of these measures was born of an ideological position and this casts light on where we find ourselves today. A good deal of this ideological thinking rests on the belief that the market and competition will deliver better service for clients and customers. Running alongside this is an antipathy to the very notion of public service and public provision. The idea, for example, that such public service and public servants are a drain on the economy, wasteful and poorly organized, permeates some areas of societal discourse, and it is reinforced by powerful political messages and certain parts of the media. Such thinking is deeply embedded in the outlook of Conservative politicians in particular, although it should not be forgotten that it was a Labour government that introduced academy schools.

Writing in 1980, two of Margaret Thatcher's favourite economists suggested that 'in schooling, the parents and child are the consumers, the teacher and school administration the producers' (Friedman and Friedman, 1980: 191). Such a perception is, in itself, the logical development from the thinking of the person acknowledged as the founding father of neoliberalism, Friedrich Hayek, who twenty years earlier stated that it is 'possible to leave the organization and management of education entirely to private efforts, with the government providing merely the basic finance and ensuring a minimum standard for all schools' (Hayek, 1960: 381). Over half a century later, this firm belief in the primacy of private provision and the disparagement of publicly provided services remains, writ large in education policy.

When we remind ourselves of what Sahlberg (2012) identifies as the five principal features of the GERM, we can see how these match-up with what has been discussed above:

- standardization of education
- a focus on core subjects
- low-risk ways of reaching learning goals
- the use of corporate management models
- test-based accountability policies.

Two important and connected considerations emerge from this discussion. First the point needs underlining that the introduction of the current apparatus of control and measurability stems from a deep-seated ideological position. The second, connected, issue is that for teachers to develop ways of resisting the GERM, it is necessary for them to see the attacks on their professional autonomy as part of a much wider political and ideological battle against the very tenets of public service and conceptions of social provision. In the final chapter I discuss how and why this is so important, if we are to do anything beyond bemoaning current circumstances.

For teachers and those with an interest in schools, it is important that we do more than analyse where we are and how we got here. It might well be excusable to slip into pessimism, in light of this sustained and deeply rooted ideological onslaught on the beliefs of many teachers. Even some 15 years ago, Stephen Ball clearly captured how this could happen:

It is difficult not to conclude that political enthusiasm for accountability and competition are threatening both to destroy the meaningfulness of 'authentic' teaching and profoundly change what it means 'to teach' and to be a teacher. The global trends of school improvement and effectiveness, performativity and management are working together to eliminate emotion and desire from teaching – rendering the teacher's soul transparent but empty.

(Ball, 1999: 9)

The testimony from teachers in this book goes some way in demonstrating that the teacher's soul is not yet empty and that notions of authenticity have not been completely eliminated. This is not to argue that the ideological hegemony of neoliberalism and marketization have had no impact on what teachers do on a daily basis. Nor is it to argue that everything in the garden of teachers' consciousness is rosy. The chapters that follow immediately, which outline how such ideology manifests itself in threatening and unwelcome ways, might seem to be a gloomy read. They are included to confirm to teachers that their own experience is far from a localized one born of the eccentricities of their school management team, but a universal one that will be recognized by colleagues, in England and elsewhere. The reader will need to remember that for all this gloom, the 'emotion and desire' are both alive and well, as subsequent chapters reveal.

Chapter 3

Speaking truth to power?
Whose voices are here?

The indomitable spirit of a teacher who will take a bland moment and turn it into an opportunity.

Max – former headteacher and teacher educator

The following chapters try to capture the experience of teachers. The basic thesis of this book is that teachers have not fallen for the ideology of the market but wish to resist the GERM. So, this is meant to be an affirmation of teachers' resilience and their commitment to children's education in the widest sense. My hope is that the book will be read by teachers, many of whom will be encouraged to know that they are far from being a lone voice – which is one of the concerns that surfaces from much of their testimony to me. I hope too that teacher educators, school leaders and parents may find this of value. They should be encouraged by what they hear from those charged with the education of their children.

The evidence for this book was gathered in two main parts. The first was in 2010–11, as part of a doctoral study about teachers' professional autonomy in England (Berry, 2013a). During that time I interviewed 22 teachers, from across all sectors, individually on two separate occasions. They also furnished me with thousands of words of written testimony, sometimes at my prompting, in relation to the rapid introduction of government initiatives during that period (Berry, 2013a). They frequently got in touch in order to present anecdotes and events at school that they thought might interest me. Alongside the views of these teachers were added those of three headteachers whose schools enjoyed varying levels of success gauged against inspection criteria, two figures close to the formulation and enactment of government policy and a leading education journalist. I then sought the views of 13 experienced teachers in December 2011, using a short questionnaire.

In 2015 I interviewed or received written testimony from a further 32 teachers on an individual basis. In two separate focus groups I recorded the views of another ten teachers. At two teacher conferences I was able to conduct group seminars with a total of another 25 teachers. Along with this have gone innumerable casual and informal conversations with teachers, a great many of whom expressed willingness to be participants and many of whom made suggestions about potentially interested respondents. This significant hinterland of evidence from teachers who were not formally interviewed is not quoted directly in the chapters that follow, although the occasional anecdote is paraphrased.

This willingness on the part of teachers to supply information unprompted has been characteristic of the evidence gathered. It has been difficult to keep pace with the offers of anecdotes, evidence and other general contributions. On hearing of this project, a fellow ex Head of English phones me and vehemently demands to be interviewed; two young teachers, who I meet briefly during a tea-break at a schools' debate, hurriedly compete to furnish me with observations on their diminishing professional autonomy; having spoken briefly about the project at a conference, teachers email me the next day with illustrative anecdotes. This level of engagement tells us something important: teachers are interested in their practice in a way that goes beyond mere fulfilment of their occupational and professional duties. What is less encouraging is that teachers bemoan the lack opportunity to discuss their practice, and this emerges as a major concern for many teachers – a topic to which we return later.

The 100-plus teachers who directly participated correspond largely to the profile of teachers in England's primary and secondary schools in terms of age, gender and ethnicity at the time of writing (DfE, 2014a). In broad terms this means that the majority of respondents were from primary schools, there were more women than men and the age profile was mainly between 25 and 45. In line with DfE figures, some 13 per cent could be categorized as not 'white British'. In the 2010–11 study I made no attempt to distinguish between the views of primary, secondary or special school teachers. The purpose was to identify the factors that had an impact on their professional autonomy and there appeared to be no specific issues that were contingent on the sector in which teachers worked. Accordingly the 2015 study, similarly, made no attempt to distinguish between the views of those working in different sectors. Where I quote their views directly, each participant has been given a pseudonym which can most easily be described as traditionally 'English'. Although corresponding to gender, this gives no indication as to ethnicity or age – any name perceived to be somewhat old-fashioned is not intended as a clue to either longevity or length of service!

So much, then, for the quantitative side of the constituency from whom testimony and response was gathered. A reader is entitled to ask: 'who were these people?' It is an important question because it would be disingenuous to suggest that they represent some scientifically constructed cross-section. If someone is interested enough to ask me about my research into the topic of teacher autonomy or the state of schools and education and then, having engaged me in conversation, volunteers herself as a respondent and subsequently suggests a colleague or friend who might add to my store of knowledge, the voices we hear are obviously not going to be those of the disengaged or uninterested.

I make no apology for the fact the voices of the cynical, the disillusioned and the time-servers – who have always existed but have been in the minority – are not represented here. Instead, we should, as a profession, pride ourselves on the fact that despite a blanket of white noise that could dispirit less hardy souls, so many teachers remain as committed, lively and energetic as they do. Teachers live in a world where a Secretary of State for Education takes space in a national newspaper to decry those who dare to question his ideas as the 'enemies of promise' (Gove, 2013). It is a discourse continued with enthusiasm by Gove's successor, who, talks of 'aggressive pressure groups who put their own interests above the best interests of children' (Morgan, 2015). Teachers inhabit a world in which the Chief Inspector of Schools tells MPs that 'if anyone tells you that staff morale is at an all-time low you will know that you are doing something right' (Parliament, 2012a). They have to endure the peculiar use of language which has meant that the simple term 'satisfactory' now means 'not good enough'.

The purpose of this book is to make space for the voice of the fully engaged but potentially dissident to be heard. Most of the voices here are those of teachers known to me through my professional life although only three are former teaching colleagues. They include former student teachers who are now in post, some teachers who have undertaken postgraduate study and some who have acted as mentors and support for those new to the profession. The majority of the teachers interviewed in 2015 were located through a 'snowballing' process of recommendations from respondents and their networks. To reiterate the point made above – offers and recommendations poured in, to the extent that it became impossible to receive testimony from all who wanted to express a view about this. GERM resistance is a live issue.

There is no pretence here about all being for the best in the best of all possible worlds. Even though England's Chief Inspector of Schools can claim at the time of writing that 'we have never had a more qualified, more motivated, more enthused generation of young teachers than we have now' (Wilshaw, 2014) he, and others, are aware there is a major problem in terms of retaining these teachers. Wilshaw himself acknowledges that 40 per cent of entrants into the profession leave within five years – a figure validated by the parliamentary select committee on education (Parliament, 2012b). And as these new entrants churn through the system, there is increasing evidence that older teachers are being discriminated against as they struggle to meet the demands of a brave new educational world (National Union of Teachers, 2015).

In terms of presenting an honest assessment of how teachers experience their working world, the testimony gathered in 2015 from teachers who had made the decision to leave the profession is also relevant. Despite widespread resistance to the GERM, its demands do diminish the spirit of some. Liam, a secondary teacher interviewed for the original study in 2010 and 2011, had left the profession by 2015. 'When people ask me (why I left) I still tell them that I loved actually teaching but not the education industry,' he explains. He talks of how he enjoyed good working relationships with colleagues and, above all, his students, but felt that school managers increasingly gave the impression that 'nothing is ever good enough'. He is proud of the fact that 'the feedback I had from children, parents and teaching assistants was fantastic', but dismayed by the way in which so many institutional demands diverted his energies away from his actual teaching. In an echo of other comments considered later, he speaks of 'disdain for the pointless marking of books for appearances' sake' and of how he likes to think of himself being more about 'relationships, not ticks'. In similar testimony from a primary teacher, Cerys talks of feeling 'cheated' into a situation where 'we stand in front of a class of children and encourage them to be passionate and inquisitive learners, when we as new teachers are being stunted in our own learning experiences' by a system that is dominated by scrutiny, checking and an unthinking adherence to policy. She ends by expressing the view that she feels 'sad that I have so much to moan about' and that she 'loved working with the children in the classroom – but that was such a minuscule part of each day that I can't see me teaching again under the current system'.

There is no denying that there are casualties. Teaching now finds itself in a situation where it loses qualified professionals and is failing to recruit at a rate that can possibly replace them (Ward, 2015). Despite these caveats, the basic premise of what follows remains the same: notwithstanding the barrage of demands that are made on teachers in England, they retain a strong sense of what education is for and how it can be a force for good. But before we look at the evidence that demonstrates this, the following chapters outline what it is that they are up against.

Chapter 4

The horror, the horror: Tested to destruction

At the end of the film *Apocalypse Now* or, if your tastes are more literary, at the end of Conrad's *Heart of Darkness*, the central figure of Kurtz, a man who has seen and done things that no human being should ever have encountered, intones the phrase, 'the horror, the horror' as he contemplates his impending demise. I'm not suggesting that life for teachers is a daily round of unspeakable cruelty and unfeeling sadism, but the unrelenting demands made on them as they pursue their everyday occupations sometimes do make it feel as though they are fending off spiteful and threatening adversaries at every turn. This feeling of vulnerability is often heightened by the very real possibility that, at any moment, their classroom door may open and in may come the clipboard wielder looking for whatever this week's 'focus on learning' may happen to be. The next chapters look at how such pressure is exerted on teachers to 'perform' in a variety of ways – often, as we shall see, against their better judgement and deeply held values. We start by contemplating the drive for results.

It is one of the principal characteristics of the Global Education Reform Movement – the GERM identified by Sahlberg and outlined in Chapter 1 – that it demands results from standardized tests as one of the means to demonstrate everything from value for money to proof of institutional progress and attractiveness in an allegedly open market. It is test and examination results that have become the sole meaningful measure by which schools define themselves both to themselves and to the outside world. In recent years, I have become increasingly taken aback when, in casual conversations with teachers about how their working lives are going, they tell me within moments about the results profile of their individual classes, departments or the school overall. As an illustration of how the importance of such examination results have become, I offer this observation from my own experience – emphasising that I do so not in the spirit of reviving a non-existent golden age, but merely to illustrate how a new culture has taken hold in a relatively short time.

As a serving practitioner I was, naturally, always interested in the results obtained by my pupils in public examinations at 16 and 18 and, as a matter of course, would break into the summer vacation when results were released to visit school. There, along with colleagues, one noted with personal and professional interest the achievements, successes and failures of our pupils and commiserated or congratulated accordingly. One then exchanged thoughts with students and colleagues and resumed the summer vacation period, generally satisfied that justice had been done, albeit alarmed by the occasional instance of either over or under-performance. Statistics relating to grades, subjects and cohorts were not collected; percentages were not collated; subject differentials were not calculated and, significantly, appeals against results were practically unheard of – the stuff of folklore. What Dale (1989) identifies as this licensed state of affairs pertained until the mid-1990s, by which time the force of the market had evolved to make the August drop-in at school a far more fraught affair for all concerned. The high-stakes nature of the tests themselves and the implications for individuals and institutions generated an atmosphere more akin to the annual meeting of a company's auditors than the staff room of a school where everyone had done their best to enhance the chances of young people. This has since developed into a situation where schools, by necessity, have garnered expertise and knowledge in terms of appeals, re-marks and the procedures required should parents and pupils wish to pursue this course. By the start of the century, part of my professional routine required me to factor-in time that would have to be spent in dealing with the appeals that increased every year. The drop-in was no longer a quick check on exam marks but a tense episode that had ramifications reaching into every corner of practice.

The drive for results stems from ideological and political choices. The Labour government of 2003 encouraged teachers to 'be creative and innovative in how they teach' but was unequivocal about the requirement to 'use *tests and targets* to help every child to develop his or her potential', which would in turn 'help the school to improve and help parents and the public to understand the *progress* of the pupils and the *performance* of the school' (Department for Education and Skills, 2003:7 *my emphases*). Apple (2004) summarizes the way in which test results became the currency in a marketized system in the following comment, worth quoting at length:

> The neoliberal emphasis ... is on making the school either part of the economy or making it into a commodity itself ... as has happened in England, where their national curriculum is sutured into the national test (the results of which are published as 'league tables' in the press and elsewhere in which schools are

compared), this provides a direct mechanism that enables the Right, in essence, to put price tags on schools and say 'This is a good school, this is a bad school.' In essence, it enables them to say 'There's no more money to support real efforts at democratic school reform, so what we need to do then is marketize.'

(Apple, 2004: 197)

In conversation with teachers about how the drive to generate results affects their daily lives, one of the most frequently expressed concerns is that although the box may be ticked, no-one is convinced that anyone has actually learnt anything. As experienced secondary teacher Steve points out, this is because so much practice, influenced by the need to 'demonstrate progress' is, of course, based on a falsehood unsupported by either educational theory or practitioners' experience:

> ... you know, we can't have every educational experience that we have with children always about meeting an objective, because sometimes you don't meet that objective, but that's not the end of the world. Other times, you might completely abandon that objective and something else will have been learned during the lesson, but the system doesn't allow for that. The system says, this is what will be learned at the beginning, you know, I mean ... that's not the way people learn, is it?

Steve's position is supported by a whole range of similar observations from teachers in the primary and secondary sectors. Harry, a secondary science teacher, talks of how a pupil 'is able to draw the diagram and that's Level 4, so OK, I'll tick it' even though he remains unconvinced that the pupil has grasped the fundamental concept of, in this case and rather aptly the human heart. Jackie, another science teacher, talks of the 'huff and puff and steam' of focusing on improving results which seems to subsume any chance of genuinely investigating a topic. Shona, a primary school teacher – and who has since left the profession – talks of how the drive for results puts 'children through the pressure for no other reason apart from the school wanting to do well in the league tables'. Of the many interesting testimonies from teachers about the sophistry of generating outcomes, among the most compelling is that of Shaun, an experienced teacher of some standing and reputation in his own school and beyond:

> We're doing a Year 7 test, and some staff are very happy with the Year 7 test, because it asks students to do three, five or seven techniques in persuasive language. So if you do three, you get a

Level, if you do five you get a Level, if you do seven you get a Level. Now that is functional. That's functional … it's functional teaching. And staff like it because they can easily mark it and assess it, because they've done three, five or seven. What it doesn't do, of course, is actually ask them to step away and say, is that any good as a piece of writing? Is it holistically persuasive? Does it really hit you? And it's that sort of functionality, I think, which has become so much the paradigm … it's easy to mark, easy to teach, that's fine. Of course what that does is narrows down the whole nature of teaching, I think, and learning.

Shaun's comments capture the mood of many responses from teachers about this functionality and from these stem two principal considerations. First is the matter of what some educationalists call the issue of 'deep learning'. In order to illuminate this point, it is instructive to consider what happens when those new to the profession come for interview for a course in teacher training (or 'teacher education' as some of us still prefer to think of it). When asked why they want to become a teacher, one of the most popular and predictable responses is a love of subject or a love of learning. These potential new entrants want to inspire and enthuse. However, the drive to produce measurable outcomes at predetermined times, irrespective of the readiness of their pupils, cuts across this desire to delve, explore or digress. Schedules of tests and requirements for results – all of which demand evidence of 'progress' – militate against these very proper ambitions and aspirations of new entrants to the profession.

Marsha, a primary school teacher – and another who has left the profession since being interviewed in 2011 – talks of how school turns into 'a sort of real boot camp' after Christmas, as test preparation for 10-year-olds dominates school life. Leanne, a secondary teacher working in a school that is on the verge of being placed into a failing Ofsted category, explains that 'the pressure to get those results' dominates her particular school and that 'I'm not entirely sure we should be pushing some of our students in that way'; such practice 'impacted my enjoyment of teaching' to the point where, in her 'darkest hours' she contemplated leaving the profession – although, given her obvious talent, I'm pleased to report that she did not do so. These comments, and the earlier observations from their colleagues, demonstrate how a discourse about learning soon becomes one about testing and quantifying. Against such a background, it is little surprise that some teachers take the line of least resistance, adopting a policy of survivalism (Ball, 2008) and where the notion of deep learning, going beyond the requirements of what is measurable, is submerged in the ensuing daily grind.

This drive for results can be a dispiriting experience for teachers who strive to ensure that genuine learning takes place. Just as alarming is the manipulation of results and data in an attempt to present outcomes in the best possible way. The practice of some schools in excluding pupils whose efforts would do little to enhance their public profile has exercised a number of parties from the Children's Commissioner to investigative journalists (Mansell, 2014). For individual teachers, the effect has been far-reaching. Secondary teachers now talk of how the Easter break is, to all intents and purposes, one unbroken series of revision sessions, often aimed at those pupils on borderline grades between a D and a C. Primary teachers describe how swathes of time are taken from the curriculum as children are prepared for tests.

In an alarming, although apparently far from isolated instance, Shona talks of how she is persuaded by her headteacher to lower grades she has awarded for an internal assessment in order to boost 'value added' scores at the end of the year. Maurice, another primary teacher, talks in a startlingly blunt way about how, when a child has been recorded as operating at a certain level, he is unabashed about neglecting that child for the time being while he attempts to enhance the performance of others in his class. Secondary teacher Donald, who has since left the profession to be an air-traffic controller – a job he considers less stressful than teaching exam classes in May – tells of instances where completed examination scripts have been weeded out and not sent for external examination. The purpose of this is to ensure that low grades or failures do not affect the school's overall results which will, of course, be in the public domain. Rather cynically, students who have taken these high-stakes examinations in good faith are told that these initial attempts now count as no more than dummy runs and so this dishonest practice on the part of the school is characterized as helpful to these young people. Other teachers confirmed their knowledge of similar instances, along with frequent testimony about practices 'helpful' to students during public examinations. The fact that cheating by teachers in the USA to improve performance in standardized tests is now so widespread that an initial internet search reveals tens of thousands of results is clear proof that the GERM really has gone viral.

In an interesting choice of analogy, two teachers who responded in 2015 opt to use the term 'Stalinist' to characterize what happens in their schools, both of which, incidentally, do well in terms of league tables and inspection results. Donald talks of how 'the Head ran the school like a

Stalinist regime, urging everyone to do anything they could to get better grades'. Clarke, a secondary teacher, believes that:

> ... targets and data rule our school as they did in Stalinist Russia. My head of department and I have started, with increasing frequency, describing our school as Stalinist in terms of obsession with production targets ... five-year plans ... and initiatives forced on us by an out-of-touch and inefficient leadership.

It is worth digressing for a moment to make a related point. None of the above is presented to argue the case that teachers should not do their level best to ensure that their charges get optimum results and grades. Teachers have always done so and have often prided themselves, and I include myself here, in teaching pupils short-cuts, tricks-of-the trade and specific techniques to squeeze every last mark that they could to improve their chances. This is not the point at issue here. When academics challenged former Education Secretary Michael Gove about the educational value of his proposed reforms to public examinations, he and his colleagues were quick to label such opposition as emanating from 'The Blob', calling such academics 'the enemies of promise'. Gove's argument was rooted in a belief that such teachers and academics, far from attempting to give children the best possible chances of success, were bloody-mindedly stuck in some woolly notions of equality and lack of challenge – a discourse that has hardly changed for over thirty years from Secretaries of State of all political persuasions. Not only does such an argument fly in the face of the efforts of those who see education as doing exactly what ministers themselves trumpet as their aim – improving the prospects for all young people – it also confuses debate with heresy. To challenge a system that has become so driven by results that it skews the learning and teaching taking place in school is not seen as expressing concern about the effect this has on everyone involved, it is deemed an affront to progress itself and an obstacle to young people's life-chances. The production of outcomes, the lifeblood of the GERM, so dominates the ideological perspective of those who arrange the school system that the views of those with knowledge, experience and first-hand research have to be denigrated at every turn.

As a final illustration for the moment, about how test results take precedence over genuine learning, I turn to an example that I first heard of from one of my student teachers some seven years ago, but which now seems to be widespread practice. It has long been the case that some secondary schools choose to enter pupils for public examinations prior to the usual age for so doing. Local and, occasionally, national newspapers revel in the tale of the 11-year-old prodigy with a hatful of GCSEs. As a Head of English dragged kicking and screaming into entering pupils for SATs at 14, I used to make the deal with them and their teachers that once the tests were over, we'd spend the rest of Year 9 doing something new, creative and experimental until the end of the year. I was naively horrified to find out that in many schools, as soon as SATS were finished, pupils at once embarked on their GCSE courses. However, even that obsession with result production now seems fairly tame in relation to the following startling story.

Having observed a (perfectly good) lesson taught by one of my student teachers I drift into general conversation with her after we have finished the official feedback. The school is one where my institution has placed many training teachers and, indeed, this student's Head of Department is an alumnus of our School of Education. My student tells me that she has a top-set Year 10 and that the school wants these children entered for GCSE in her subject at the first possible opportunity. In this case it had been the January of Year 10 and some had been successful in their efforts. I ask her what she does with these successful students and it transpires that she does nothing because these students are deemed to have finished with her subject – English – once a grade C has been obtained. They are now to concentrate on other subjects, ensuring as far as possible that more grade Cs are obtained, so that the school – and, by the by, the pupils – garner as much GCSE success as possible. So, just to be clear, at the tender age of 14, pupils who, let us remember, have done well enough to pass an exam at a very early stage in their education, are done with English. Or Maths. Or whatever other quick-fix examination result they can be used for to grab outcomes for the data machine.

Donald amplifies this story when talking of his own experience:

> The school, in an attempt to get a head-start on the league tables against other schools in the area, made a lot of Year 11s who had taken either History or Geography take both exams. This was achieved by pulling them from RE classes and Citizenship, and instead making them do History or Geography. The Head of Geography was in despair because she had been told in January that she had to teach the entire GCSE curriculum to a group of Year 11s by May.

The aspiration to provide broad and balanced curriculum thus becomes little more than an exercise in getting as many good examination results as a school can muster. One of the features of how standardization and measurability have been allowed to become pre-eminent in educational discourse is the way in which teacher training courses and schemes have often been reduced to narrow survival tips alongside inculcation into the culture and habits of any particular school. Robin Alexander, an academic once so trusted by government that he was one of the 'three wise men' charged with formulating primary school policy in England in 1992, characterized this as a 'what works' approach (Alexander, 2004; 2010). When reflecting on the earlier concerns of Simon in 1981 about the lack of pedagogical understanding in England's schools, he argues that 'the prominence of curriculum in English educational discourse has meant that we have tended to make pedagogy subsidiary' to the business of completing what any given curriculum may require (2004: 11). As a result, debate and investigation about pedagogical matters is reduced to nothing more than a consideration – and usually an acceptance of – 'what works'.

This view of what teaching and learning can be reduced to is underpinned by the notion that education is merely what Paulo Freire (whose works are, regrettably, uncharted territory for most new teachers) called a depositing exercise:

> … in which students are the depositories and the teacher is the depositor. Instead of communication, the teacher issues communiqués and 'makes deposits' which the students patiently receive, memorize and repeat.
>
> (Freire, 1990: 45).

It then follows that for teachers, doing their job should be an easy enough business – depositing or delivering whatever works and which needs to be introduced to young people. Teaching, therefore, becomes 'a techno-rational activity, the underlying mechanics of which can be revealed through appropriate research and then universally applied in the classroom' (Davies and Edwards, 1999: 269).

Hugh Busher (2006) captures how this 'works' in the following way:

> In the neoliberal and quasi-economic framework that dominates national discourses about society and about education as part of that, knowledge seems to be defined as a product from a factory process (like a computer) called schooling rather than a sense-making process through which people create understandings of the different worlds around them.
>
> (Busher, 2006: 107)

Teachers, however, become only too well aware that worthwhile learning is not about acts of depositing and that although they can develop a repertoire of ideas, resources and approaches that become pretty reliable, dealing with young people defies any sure-fire, instrumentalist approach. Children are not products and neither is knowledge. Beyond this, the very idea that fourteen-year-olds might have exhausted their curiosity about anything from words to numbers, to science, to design, is not only plainly preposterous but also paints a desperate picture of what happens to learning when all that matters is the test result.

What does this mean for the students themselves? In an interview with Darlene, a secondary teacher with over twenty years of experience, she talks of how she has never before encountered so much stress and unhappiness among the young people in her school. In a similar vein, Laura, another secondary teacher with significant experience, speaks of how students tell her that they think many staff have become tired, demoralized and 'just not as much fun', and say to her 'why should we bother? Everyone's leaving.' When I meet Merryn Hutchings to talk about her report into the effects of the accountability agenda on children's well-being (Hutchings, 2015), she expresses genuine astonishment at the findings of her research which reveal this distancing of pupils from their teachers. 'I was truly shocked. Teachers were telling me things like "I just don't know the children – I don't have time to get to know the children. I don't have enough time to notice them."'

In a theme that appears frequently in teachers' testimonies, regret is expressed at the way in which children themselves have become 'grade-junkies'. Holly, who feels that 'we've turned into data-monkeys ... who spend our lives monitoring children as if they were pieces of material', says that although she is 'not interested (in grades) and I tell the kids that, they're still desperate to know what' the grade is. Such comments are typical of those of many respondents, particularly in the secondary sector. Belinda, new to the profession, talks of how she is 'dispirited by kids who have learnt to chase and cherish their grades'. Many respondents talk of how it is far from uncommon for children to ask what the learning objective of the lesson is, should the teacher have failed or chosen not to identify it at the start of the session.

In her report, Merryn Hutchings points to extensive research which reveals that in England:

> The most obvious impact of the pressure on children and young people has been in emotional responses: it has been widely reported that children are showing increasing levels of anxiety, disaffection and mental-health problems.
>
> (Hutchings, 2015: 55)

The same report concludes that the measuring mechanisms currently used are 'deeply damaging to children and young people' and do not 'foster the skills and talents that are needed in higher education, employment or the attributes that will be valued in future citizens' (Hutchings, 2015: 7). The savage irony here is that even in pursuit of a 'what works' agenda, where outcomes and production are paramount, the constant quest for good results doesn't even do what it's supposed to do. While increasing the levels of anxiety in teachers and young people alike, the pursuit of test scores, even where they 'have increased ... does not necessarily reflect children's underlying level of knowledge, understanding and skills' (Hutchings, 2015: 66).

In an alarming coda to these findings, a report from the Children's Society of 2015 also found that school life in general for children in England compared poorly with that for their international counterparts:

> In particular, England ranked 14th for children's satisfaction with their relationship with their teachers and also 14th for agreeing that teachers treated them fairly (although ninth for feeling that teachers listened). England also ranked in the bottom third of countries for satisfaction with other children at school, things learned, the school experience in general and liking going to school.
>
> (Children's Society, 2015: 41)

Those whom the gods would destroy they first make mad, so the classical saying goes. As Kurtz nears his end, having left behind him a trail of destruction so devastating that it defies comprehension, the reader or viewer is left thinking that madness of some sort has contributed to his fall. It is the GERM, and the market forces that sustain it, that is responsible for the madness that says to young people that their knowledge of the great concepts is to be ended with the gaining of an arbitrary grade for which they have been systematically coached and rehearsed. Fortunately, as later chapters demonstrate, there is an antidote to the lunacy that so degrades learning that it becomes nothing more than a narrow route to success in tests.

Chapter 5

You lookin' at me? Or *qui custodiet ipsos custodes*?

I've chosen the Latin phrase – it means 'who will watch the watchmen?' – not only because it captures the spirit of this chapter, but also because of its resonance with my own education. As a beneficiary of the 11-plus system, I was sent from an ordinary neighbourhood primary school to the great unknown land (for myself and my family, at any rate) of a boys' grammar school. There I was introduced to a whole range of new experiences, most of which I just got on with, tolerated or even enjoyed. One of these novelties was Latin. There is any number of arguments about the benefits or disadvantages of learning Latin but I don't believe it's done me any perceptible harm at all. That, however, is not the point of my mentioning it here.

I refer to it because of the conduct of my various Latin teachers, which, in itself, was a reflection of the conduct of pretty well all those who taught me. All my teachers were men, all were university graduates and, in a reflection of the times, many had seen active military service of some sort. As a consequence, the majority of them were not to be unnerved by the antics of even the most precocious or bold of the adolescents who crossed their path – which is not to say that there were never any hopeless cases whose lives we rendered miserable. But when your book was marked, it was ticked as being right or wrong, tossed back to you and that was that. I recently read my school report for 1968, the entire wordage of which would not now measure up to the content of a single subject in most contemporary school reports. The idea that a fellow professional would enter the sanctum of any of my teachers' classrooms to pronounce on their performance, much less trot through to check a few items on a list, would have been condemned as the stuff of improbable fiction.

I am not suggesting that such unbridled autonomy was the mark of a better, brighter world. What I am doing is painting a picture of schools where teachers acted with a degree of certainty that they were doing the right thing. Dale's (1989) notion of licensed autonomy, teachers' freedom to act as they felt best as long as anything egregious was avoided and public examination results and, in the case of a grammar school, university entrance were achieved, fits perfectly here. To the teacher in the second decade of the twenty-first century, such freedom and trust are practically unknown.

This chapter – the last of the gloom – looks at the way in which the concepts of accountability, scrutiny and management, all central characteristics of the GERM, have come to play a prominent part in the day-to-day lives of all teachers.

It is important to start with a clear statement: most teachers are entirely relaxed about accountability. Interviewed in 2015, Darlene offers the unprompted comment that 'I have no problem with being accountable. I'm a public servant; it's what I signed up for'. She goes on to say, however, that what she now has to tolerate is 'perverse accountability, irrational accountability'. Nonetheless, in her firm acceptance of the notion of accountability, she is entirely in tune with her fellow respondents. The original cohort of 22 interviewees, first interviewed in 2010, were asked an initial question about what they thought it was to be a professional teacher. All but three responded within seconds by talking of their responsibility to their students and their parents. The three who did not do so were all in senior positions – and they spoke of their accountability towards teachers for whom they had managerial responsibility. Many talked about how their notions of social responsibility informed their actions, with over half talking in terms of being role models for children and young people. For some it was their personal faith that informed this strong sense of accountability. The overarching sense of doing the right thing by their students is captured neatly by Laura, part of the original cohort but interviewed again in 2015, who expresses the view that for her the fundamental purpose of her job remains unchanged: 'providing an education that suits the needs of the children who come through our door, regardless of government procedure and policies'.

The way in which Laura draws a correspondence between what she feels to be the purpose of her job and the manner in which government actions can present obstacles to this is an important one. The actions and pronouncements of 'the government' feature frequently in almost all testimony, written and spoken, from these respondents in all the periods of data collection. It is, however, important to make the point here that none of the criticism and, quite frequently, the anger directed towards those in office is ever made in party-political terms. It is true that certain prominent figures – Michael Gove, Michael Wilshaw and the late Chris Woodhead – are often singled out for commentary that is less than complimentary. However, respondents almost never talk about such figures in terms of their political affiliations or possible party connections. Rather they are seen, almost universally, as out-of-touch with schools, teachers and young people. One observation that features in a great many responses is a genuine curiosity as to why ministers and their advisers have never themselves been teachers. The last Secretary of State to have been a teacher – and she was the first to have done so in a comprehensive school – was Estelle Morris who held the office for a year as Labour minister from 2002 to 2003. In a group conversation with primary teachers, one of their number expresses frustration with 'the constant discourse of everything being awful' and asks why government 'doesn't explore what's already there and build on the positive'. Secondary teacher Jean complains that 'they don't trust us at the end of the day, do they? Otherwise they'd have teachers in the government.'

Central to the question of how teachers feel about government is a perception on their part that there is an element of double-speak in the messages politicians send to them. The coalition government of 2010–15 acted as quickly as any administration to introduce measures to facilitate the privatization of the education system – but as it did so, it also chose to promote a message of teacher independence and freedom (Berry, 2013b). Michael Gove promised teachers that he would 'give you freedom to teach how you want to' (Berry, 2013b: 273). Respondents were unimpressed by this apparently emollient move. Three teachers with significant experience express their reservations. Max comments that:

> I don't think he (Gove) understands the word autonomy; I don't think he understands what he's talking about in that sense. I think autonomy … when I hear the word autonomy, my understanding is: teachers who are empowered to do the job they see fit best, and they have the skills to do it. I think that the system he's thinking of is not that.

His sentiment is echoed by Christine when she says that 'you are only allowed to do what you're allowed to do by the political agenda … and the direction which the government decides schools need to go or education needs to go'. David, a leading member of a major teachers' organization, dubs this the 'Govian paradox':

> And there's this idea yes, we want autonomy, we want everyone to be free to do what they like, but you've got to teach phonics; you've got to do the EBacc, you've got to do all these things, and it isn't freedom, and that is the problem.

Finally on this topic, Shaun summarizes many responses when he observes that:

> So whilst you say that teachers are free to teach what they want in their own direction, unfortunately the direction's already set in stone and therefore you have to just arrive at the destination that somebody else has made for you.

Teachers live happily with the responsibility they bear to their students, but it is a different story when it comes to the government whose actions, demands and ambitions they find ill-informed, inconsistent and irritating. This irritation is compounded by having to live with another feature of the GERM: corporate management models. Principal among the features of this is the need to scrutinize production, outcome and practices. For teachers in England in 2015, this management manifests itself in three main ways: inspections from the Office for Standards in Education (Ofsted); the high-stakes, performance-management related lesson observation and, lastly, the 'learning walk'.

It was the Conservative government of John Major that introduced Ofsted in 1992. In many ways, of course, this body, which in its inspectoral role replaced Her Majesty's Inspectorate (HMI), was the logical consequence of the events set in train by Callaghan in 1976 and pursued through Thatcher's Education Reform Act (ERA) of 1988. HMI inspections were characterized by an element of professional advice, even suggestions for development, as well as pointing out faults and problems (Chapman, 2002). Ofsted's role was unequivocally inspectoral. The reasoning is unimpeachable – *if* one accepts a view of education as a marketable commodity: schools need to produce material, certain workers are charged with managing and controlling this process and, naturally, the rate of production needs to be measured, inspected and compared to that of competitors. Ofsted, the body charged with this inspection process has permeated the consciousness of schools, teachers, students, parents and the general public in a way that few public bodies could have done in the past. A measure of its prominence in the lives of teachers is revealed in the first interviews conducted in 2010–11. Although the term is never mentioned in any of the interview prompts, which talk about trust, autonomy and pressures, not one teacher failed to mention Ofsted – often within moments of being asked about trust. In all of the data gathered in 2015, only three teachers do not mention Ofsted in their comments – again, with the term not introduced in the questions or prompts. For almost all of them, their view of the inspection system still corresponds to Michael Fielding's observation of some years ago that 'the system for inspecting schools in England carries with it an over-confident and brusque carelessness born of too much power, too much questionable data and too little thought' (Fielding, 2001: 695).

The basic argument of this book is that teachers' spirits have not been crushed by the unremitting demands of educational reform. So it's right to start by giving room to voices of defiance and dissent when it comes to Ofsted. This is best summed up in a comment from a primary teacher whose school had been favourably judged in its latest inspection. Speaking with the approval of colleagues in a group discussion, he declares that 'we don't think they're useful. They don't do anything meaningful.' Similarly, Malcolm, a teacher in a special school who has just received an 'outstanding' individual assessment, is unimpressed by the process: 'I didn't do anything different and if I had done something different, it would probably have gone wrong'. Darlene, an experienced secondary teacher talks of how she still did 'mad things' when Ofsted came in, much to the concern of her colleagues and senior managers, but still got 'outstanding'. Charles talks of how he 'can turn it on when they come in if I want to'. What is interesting is that all of these respondents – and they are typical of many – might have been expected to have thought well of a process in which they achieved obvious personal success. The opposite is true. All of these teachers were contemptuous of a process that they considered intrusive and unhelpful.

The reasons for this antipathy are telling. One could argue that no worker in any occupation welcomes inspection and scrutiny, so why should teachers be so precious about being observed and graded? The argument here centres on the fact that one-off drop-ins to lessons – as we see later when considering the prevalence of the 'learning walk' – can only offer a narrow and limited amount of real evidence on which to base judgements, the outcomes of which can have profound implications in the age of performance-related pay and data-driven decision making. Beyond these considerations, the underpinning theory behind this process, if we can glorify this inspectoral approach with such a term, is that somewhere there are 'perfect' lessons, the quality and nature of which can be preserved and replicated and used elsewhere. The following testimony, which again is typical of much comment gathered from teachers, provides convincing rebuttal to such lazy thinking.

Abigail has recently retired after over thirty years of service in primary schools in inner-city areas. Her story is best told in her own words, presented to me in written form:

> The term before I retired, the deputy head in her role as teaching
> and learning coordinator came to do a lesson observation (my

last one). At the end of the lesson she put down her clipboard and said, 'I can't find a single fault. That was more than outstanding. That was such an amazing lesson I want you to do it again tomorrow so we can video it. It can be a record of the outstanding teaching we have in school and be used for training. Ofsted will be impressed and we will benefit from your expertise after you are gone.'

My refusal did not go down too well and in fact she approached me several times before I felt the need to spell it out. That lesson was gone and could not be 'done again'. It didn't follow a prescribed path, it responded to the needs of that group of children at that point in time. I like to think that the many occasions that I supported new and trainee teachers in their classrooms and welcomed them to take part in my lessons, helped them in a way that sitting passively in front of a video and being told 'this is how to teach' never could. As for forming part of 'evidence' for Ofsted, forget it. What I really wanted to put across was that all teachers are unique with their own qualities and strengths and their own way of inspiring their pupils. The constant observations with the tick-sheet mentality can stifle innovation and enthusiasm and encourage some teachers to deliver 'safe' lessons. Fortunately I always did well in lesson observations but that was because I always stuck to my way of doing things and never felt the need to 'perform'.

What these dissenting voices have in common is an appreciation of the concept of performativity, even though the term itself may not be familiar to all these respondents (see Chapter 2 and Ball, 2008). Although Ofsted may seem to be all-pervasive – and it is as powerful in its absence as in its presence, as schools wait in a state of constant expectation of 'the call' confirming their selection for inspection – there are many who refuse to be quelled or intimidated by it. In many cases it is because teachers have thought critically and analytically about a system that has no sound pedagogical foundation.

For all of this feisty distrust of the process, the quest for the 'outstanding' rating at either individual or institutional level has become something of a Holy Grail for many teachers and their managers. Schools proudly string up banners on perimeter fences to announce this level of success; many display selected quotations from Ofsted reports on posters in the school corridors and open spaces. In a marketized situation in which parents, allegedly, have a choice of schools (see Burgess *et al.*, 2011), it is unsurprising that such validation is sought even if, paradoxically, it is from an organization that many in the profession distrust and dislike.

Given their experiences of Ofsted, any hostility is not at all surprising. Laura's resigned compliance captures that of many other respondents when she asks 'what hoops are we going to have to go through to get them to leave us alone for a couple of years?' An experienced primary teacher talks in a group discussion about her utter contempt for a process that identifies her as both 'good' and 'requires improvement' in the same lesson. The experience of newly qualified secondary teacher Clarisse is also typical:

> In March (2015) our school undertook a 'Mocksted' in preparation for Ofsted this summer. The school's management team went crazy, teachers became headless chickens; the caretaker was given a list of 'fix-its' as long as his arm. What I'm trying to say is that we were scared. We worried about the result of an experience we had set up. We feared the system we had chosen to be in. Seems ridiculous, doesn't it?

The fear and anxiety of which Clarisse speaks runs through a good deal of the testimony gathered. To this I add an illustrative episode of my own.

I am sitting in my university office at 5 p.m. on a November evening. I am waiting to see one of my master's students, a maths teacher in a local secondary school who has just embarked on his final dissertation. His appointment was at 4.45 but, as a former schoolteacher, I am well aware of the many things that may have delayed this young man at the end of the school day. At about 5.15 he bounds up the stairs offering a breathless apology. I reassure him that I have not been put out, he thanks me and then explains: 'It's Ofsted'. I hold up my hand in a gesture of understanding, demonstrating that I recognize the impact of an impending visit and ask him when it will be – expecting him to tell me that it will be within the next few days. His look tells me that I have misunderstood. 'Oh, it's not now,' he tells me. 'We reckon it'll be some time in June.' I forbear to ask him why a special meeting, for that is what has delayed him, has been held about an event that may, possibly, take place some eight months hence, but I only have to remind myself of the fractiousness engendered by Ofsted, experienced in my own schools and those of my respondents, to leave the question unasked.

I am giving the final words on Ofsted to Kim, interviewed in 2010 at the start of what has, so far, been a successful teaching career. Her experiences typify much of what others told me or wrote about and so merit citing at some length. I have done so by reproducing the verbatim transcript of Kim's spoken testimony which, I hope, helps to convey some of the disappointment and disillusionment caused by what happened to her:

> I found … after the whole experience, after they'd come in, I felt really deflated from it. I think it took me about four to six weeks until I felt happy again. We had them in for two days just after half-term, so we had the October half-term; then they came in on the Wednesday–Thursday. We got told on the Monday, and it was a real shock, coming back after half-term and then they were coming in, so I'd prepared all my lessons and an inspector came and saw me with my top set Year 9 which I'm so thankful for. It could have been a much worse class. But then afterwards, after he saw me, I really felt proud of my lesson. I felt the kids, they were amazing. They really performed well, they were working really hard, but after the session when I saw him, he said that it was a good lesson, and I asked him how could it be outstanding? What would I need to do, and he said to me, 'oh that's not my job to tell you'. And I just found that a really frustrating process, how, you know, he can sit at the back and he can judge me, but there's no thing about me, to develop, there's nothing about … it seems to feel negative, what you haven't done, but in the sense of really broad criticisms, whereas nothing about, oh this was good but perhaps if you did this, it would be outstanding, and it just … it just felt really negative and then at the end of the whole Ofsted inspection, we could only get a satisfactory anyway, because of the exam results. So that was a really … I just found the whole experience, if they could only give us satisfactory anyway, what was the point of them coming in? It just felt quite a frustrating process and, yeah, I did feel a bit deflated after that and a bit annoyed. And I don't think it was until I came back after Christmas that I actually started enjoying teaching again.

If teachers maintain a distrust of Ofsted, which has become almost historical, then this discomfort has become matched in recent years as schools have become adept at exerting their own, home-grown forms of scrutiny and control. Students of political thought may hear echoes of Gramsci's idea of cultural hegemony here, when he talks of how dominant power 'not only justifies and maintains its domination but manages to win the active consent of those over whom it rules' (Gramsci, 1971: 245). The development of this in-house control and scrutiny is best illustrated in a group conversation with teachers, one of whom tells of how, at the start of her career some thirty years ago, she made plenty of mistakes and misjudgements, most of which were either tolerated by senior staff who remembered such failings themselves or who were happily prepared to let her learn from the experience. A younger colleague listens with some envy, telling of how in the first eight months of her career she has had to endure at least five formal observations, each of which, it is made clear to her, could have an impact on the incremental progression of her salary. Anecdotal evidence is now also rife about the use of formulaic lesson observations, carried out using predetermined criteria in an inflexible way to undermine experienced staff, many of whom take the option of leaving the profession rather than embark on procedures that they regard as ignominious and insulting.

If the internal lesson observation represents the triumph of a managerial model in education, it does, at least, have the advantage, in the view of many respondents, of being something that can be prepared for, and a safe, compliant lesson planned accordingly. The same cannot be said of the now ubiquitous 'learning walk', when managers walk around the school at times of their choosing checking that all in-house requirements, regulations and rules are being adhered to by teachers. On the surface, such events should be both innocuous and helpful. Indeed, as an experienced member of staff I used to do a few myself; the difference being that when I did so, I was genuinely checking to see if colleagues were doing OK and, if not, what I, or anyone else, might do to help. This will sound quaint to the contemporary teacher. Donald now sees such events as 'a punitive exercise to harangue teachers' and Martin regards them as part of the 'dark, unbelievably stupid side of teaching'.

I have seen training teachers formulaically 'delivering' a script at the start and end of lessons and have stopped asking them why they are doing so: they are ensuring that, in the case of an unexpected visit, they are complying with their school's particular expectations. Belinda, a newly qualified secondary teacher, tells me of a situation in which standard PowerPoint templates have to be used for every lesson. When I press her on how this happens in lessons where children may be active, on their feet or discussing a topic, she informs me that this is immaterial – the templates, which cover such matters as lesson objectives and a summary of the learning, *must* be used. What is more, it is 'non-negotiable' that something must be written in the students' books to show what has been done – a theme to which we will return. Just to ensure that Belinda does not go off-message, the school has issued her with a lanyard on which these non-negotiables have been inscribed. She cheerily admits to me, however, that she has 'lost' hers.

The learning walk – an expression identified as 'Orwellian' by three respondents – is widely viewed as a means of spot-checking by managers. In the application of this brusque device, the idea of 'learning' is reduced to compliance with a set of indicators, expectations and actions which are mechanically applied as the required indicators and will, in turn, apparently lead to the acquisition of knowledge and understanding. These indicators are then, literally, ticked off on lists as having been achieved. Quite where such a view of learning sits in the great tradition of Bruner, Vygotsky, Piaget and Freire is an idea that is probably best left unexamined; Brian Simon's 1981 question about the lack of pedagogy hangs in the air.

Along with the learning walk goes the book-trawl, to inspect the level of 'marking'. These trawls require that teachers present the exercise books of their students to school managers on a regular basis so that their marking can be inspected. It is worth stating from the start that teachers expect to mark children's work: it's a centrally important and vital part of what they do. It can be time-consuming, onerous and, on occasion, stultifyingly boring but, to cite an idea referred to above, it is an absolute 'non-negotiable'. The marking and assessment of work per se is not the cause of teachers' complaints. Their concern resides in their understanding that school-leaders, looking to demonstrate progress and achievement, are desperately looking for units of measurement with which to do so. Often, this is aligned to a wish for institutional uniformity of approach so that there will be no confusion on the part of students as to where they stand and what they need to do to reach the next level – I borrow the language of managers here. The upshot of this, as Belinda observes, is that 'it's not just the books being marked, it's you being marked'.

Belinda, like many respondents, is charged with ensuring that there is something written in books for every lesson, whether or not it has been relevant to do so. And certain codes, phraseology and signals have to be used consistently. Primary teacher Cerys writes about her experience, typical of many others:

> As for a marking policy, we had five different coloured pens, three A4 pages of code to use and we spent three staff meetings (six hours) discussing it. I ask myself, what Year 4 gives a hoot about seeing P, A or I in their book!

The point at issue here is not just, as one member of a group discussion puts it, that managers succeed only in 'wearing the whole school to a frazzle with their anxiety about indicators', it is that there is no pedagogical or organizational justification for such an approach. If ever there was encouragement for teachers to adopt what is commonly dubbed a 'tick and flick' approach, then this insistence on the slavish application of specific devices, rather than looking for evidence of understanding, or identifying the need for help and assistance, then this is it. I have had school leaders tell me that the book-trawl is a good way to catch out the lazy and to warn the slacker. In reply, I have pointed out to them that one of the first things I talk to beginning teachers about is the avoidance of the collective punishment for the individual misdemeanour; it seems to be a lesson lost on those wielding power over their fellow teachers.

Pedagogically, the book-trawl makes no sense. As we see in later chapters, one great joy of teaching lies in following the moment, letting things flow and allowing genuine learning to take place. Secondary teacher of history Charles captures this perfectly when he says 'if you're in the middle of a great discussion about the Holocaust, you don't just say "right, that's ten minutes up, let's write something down"'. The 'need' to write something in books militates against everything learning is about and leads to even more serious implications: Martin talks about how he and colleagues plan work and schemes in order to minimize the amount of written work undertaken by the students, whether or not they believe that academically this is the right thing to do. 'We engineer the work to reduce the marking', he tells me, then relating a bizarre anecdote. In a Year 9 English class he has some enthusiastic writers. The book-trawlers insist that every page of a child's book must have some teacher comment – a simple tick is insufficient. Some children are capable of writing some 25 pages in their exercise books on one exercise. Martin's dilemma is clear. He likes to think that he has been instrumental in inspiring this writing; he wants the children to do this and to read their work. In practical terms, he knows that he cannot comment on every page in detail … but it is incumbent on him to do so. His teacher instincts cannot possibly allow himself to dissuade the children from writing. Expediency is not an option, even following discussion with school managers. Martin, whom I interviewed in 2015 and who my experienced eye recognizes as an extremely able teacher, has now left to teach overseas.

Teachers and the general public are treated to regular media interest about falling academic standards. So it is unsurprising that schools have become obsessed – I use the term carefully – with demonstrating how they are improving or achieving such standards. Their future depends on doing so. Darlene, outspoken and highly accomplished, talks of how she is in a position where she can challenge her headteacher about how the application of the methods of scrutiny – the high-stakes observation, the learning walk, the book-trawl – are having a detrimental effect on herself and her colleagues. 'The head gets out a graph, shows me the data and tells me that unless we do this, we're out of a job,' she tells me. Although she is unconvinced by the argument, Darlene knows that others will be less confident in their opposition. In summary the scrutiny applied to teachers can provoke outcomes that are rather grotesque: lessons are planned to minimize written outcomes; teachers mark work not simply for the benefit of children but to watch their own backs; 'scripts' are delivered in lessons (even though they have become meaningless as children hear them repeated constantly) and the quest for 'higher standards' – without ever examining what this means other than improved grades – becomes an overwhelming demand.

It is school managers who carry out this scrutiny. A number of respondents, particularly in the 2015 interviews and commentaries, chose to mention the role of these colleagues in the process. Not all are as dismissive as Holly, who calls them 'puppets'. Some broadly agree with Laura who concedes that 'these are intelligent people, they don't actually believe all of this'. The most colourful testimony comes from Clarke, whose written comment captures some of his ire:

> I understand that these features of our school are not necessarily because our leadership are malicious individuals. Rather they are a combination of being inept, lacking in people skills and human empathy, out of touch with their staff and also under pressure from our current twisted education system, itself gripped by a psychotic accountability agenda for teachers. What I do hold against our leadership, however, is their lack of solidarity with fellow educators. For all our Head's flaws, he was a teacher once, and at the start of every term shares some new insight from a book on education he has read. And he says he's an educator, not a business manager.

The rising importance of the manager in public services is familiar to workers in a whole range of occupations. What it is vital to understand is that an ideology that puts objectives, monitoring and accountability at the centre of a system must, somehow, requisition the support of those within it to manage themselves – to convince themselves that these measures of control and scrutiny are somehow beneficial to them. The French philosopher Jean-François Lyotard explains this with great precision when he talks of the way in which such systems 'make individuals "want" what the system needs in order to perform well' (Lyotard, 1984: 62). It may be of little comfort to the classroom teacher struggling with the latest directive from an equally bewildered middle-manager that he or she is stuck in the middle of an ideological battle for the primacy of ideas, but given that what is happening to teachers is happening to almost every public-sector worker in England, there is no avoiding the fact that such a battle is taking place.

Do teachers speak out against the scrutiny that bedevils much of their working lives? The final chapter of this book explores the ways in which teachers' collective organization needs to be harnessed to beat the effects of the GERM. On an individual, day-to-day level, many teachers, to borrow Michael Apple's phrase, 'try to better conditions (for their students) in what are often small and stumbling ways ... to make (their) institutions a bit more humane, a bit more educative' (Apple, 2004: 212). The will to do so is a common feature in the comments of most respondents. But many deplore the way in which the space to discuss how to do so in a collective way has been closed down, both literally and metaphorically. The collective staffroom in many schools is now a thing of the past; respondents talk of it being 'like the Marie Celeste' and make much reference to the fact that there is simply 'no time to chat in school'. Holly, among many, observes that any such conversation about education now only takes place out of school. Belinda's comment is typical: if she does have time for lunch, it is with 'a pen in one hand and a fork in the other at my desk'. Charles relays the story of how 'a woman came in to talk to us about well-being and told us to take a walk in the lovely fields around the school at lunchtime' and was greeted with snorts of derision. When it comes to expressing opposition or dissent, Darlene and Holly, both very experienced, pride themselves on speaking in open forums, confident that their standing and accomplishment provide a degree of invulnerability. More typically, younger teacher Belinda remarks that 'all the dissenting voices have pretty well gone – we're about 70 to 80 per cent new staff'. Cerys comments that she 'would try to speak up in meetings' and that afterwards colleagues would tell her they agreed 'but most were so scared they would lose their job or look inadequate or [not] get their annual salary increment, so they chose to keep their mouths closed'.

The GERM, nurtured by those who have created the conditions for its growth, has a good deal going for it. Standardized procedures, low-risk ways to achieve narrow learning goals, corporate management and test-based accountability – all backed up with a well-developed apparatus of observation and scrutiny – might make it seem as though the odds are stacked against any assault on its primacy. Readers who leave this volume here could be excused of their pessimism, if that were the case. Fortunately, as we are about to see, antidotes are possible.

Chapter 6

Ten teaching tales to brighten the gloom: Hosepipes, the Enigma code and the execution of Anne Boleyn

In the late 1990s, during one of the periodic episodes of concern over teacher shortages, a series of adverts appeared on TV on the theme of 'Everyone remembers a good teacher'. Various celebrities, actors, sportspeople and others appeared, to extol the virtues of a Mr Smith or Miss Brown who had done something to influence their lives. All very charming. I have to say that one of the delights of a lifetime in teaching is having conversations with former pupils when I'm out and about, even though they usually have to remind me who they are. Invariably they will launch into a memory of a school play, a trip out, a barmy thing that I did in a lesson or encouraged pupils to do and even, from time to time, thank me for putting them on to an author, a film-maker or, best of all, giving them the confidence to try different things in their lives. The characters on the TV adverts did much the same thing, remembering instances that had been prompted by teachers, that inspired or influenced them. Yet I have to observe that in all of my experience or, apparently, that of those celebrities enthused by good teachers, I have never heard anyone say something like, 'That Mrs Smith – she was some teacher! She really knew how to deliver the National Curriculum'. That's because prescription has nothing to do with good teaching. It is in the spaces between what needs to be done and what actually happens in classrooms that real learning often takes place. This book exists to give prominence to those tens of thousands of teachers who maintain a strong sense of what great education can do and what it could look like on a daily basis. So here are ten tales of varying length to reaffirm to ourselves that this is what teachers do best and that this is how children learn, albeit that many of the narrators of these tales still talk of keeping a metaphorical eye on the classroom door, lest they be caught-out in their digressions! In relaying these narratives, I often leave the teachers to speak for themselves.

Tale 1: Helen and the Enigma code breaker

Early in her first interview, Helen, a teacher of maths in a secondary school, muses about 'an ideal world … where there's no more exams and you just teach and they're interested and engrossed'. It is worth making the point that Helen herself achieves good grades and results from her classes, but she remains resentful of the constant pressure and, in her view, the unnecessary reminders of the need to produce such outcomes. 'But it's the evidence, isn't it, you know?' she tells me. 'Kids enjoy my lessons. I know they do. But it's not that that people look at. It's your results, and that's what you've got – you've got to deliver'. She tells me about an episode with her Year 8 class. Somehow, she has strayed – or, to be frank, allowed herself to be led – to talking about code-breaking and because she has a keen interest in the breaking of the Enigma code during the Second World War, begins to talk about it to the class.

I hope that every teacher who reads this can recall glad memories of what happens next. The class is fascinated. They begin to ask *genuine* questions. They want to know about something that is new and exciting. And these are golden moments for both the class and the teacher: the class is happy not to be doing any 'real work' and the teacher is being happily – and knowingly – diverted from routine business. But a seam has been opened and the sensible teacher knows she must mine it, whether or not it matches today's Learning Objective staring down at her from the interactive whiteboard. Before anyone knows it, they have reached the end of the lesson and a good time has been had by all.

Regrettably for Helen, she feels a sting in the tail. She says she knows that she has genuinely excited interest and, if need be, could argue that there is ample mathematical content in what she has talked about. Nonetheless, she ends this explanation by reflecting in a rather poignant but sardonic way that the digression 'took up a lesson … I wasted a lesson, that's how it was at the end of the day. Oh my God, I've got to catch up. I've got to finish this chapter.' Although I strive to be as neutral as possible in my capacity as researcher and interviewer, I admit to breaking my own rules on this occasion by letting Helen know that no one in their right mind could have regarded her actions in such a light. Even though she broke away for a while, Helen shows herself not to be GERM free. The same applies to Robert.

Tale 2: Robert, the conkers and why your mum is always right

Robert is a primary teacher in east London. During an interview conducted in autumn, he tells how a child found a conker on the way to school and took it into a class that contains 'children who don't know what a conker is'. His immediate dilemma is to decide whether or not to talk to the class about conkers or to press on with the numeracy lesson scheduled for that morning, which is part of the school's prescribed procedure. He ponders for a few moments before deciding, against his instinctive judgement, to postpone the conkers to later in the day. Unsurprisingly, by the time he gets round to doing so the children have predictably lost 'some of their enthusiasm'. The moment has been lost and Robert has learnt a lesson of his own – but not before he has also received a reprimand of his own as well.

As a coda to the story he relates how he speaks about this to his mother, a retired Deputy Head, who gently tells him off and advises him in future, to 'change everything around ... and focus on what had been brought in'. When asked whose approach is better, he is unequivocal that it is 'my mum'. He is convinced that if he were allowed to follow such instincts and not be bound by externally imposed constraints his students would learn more, 'get far more out of' school and be further inspired to explore and investigate. Although neither of us mentions it at the time, it is fair to point out that Robert's mum worked in a much more autonomous, less regulated age.

Tales 3 and 4: Amy and Miss Havisham, Arthur and Anne Boleyn

I have often used the tales of the Enigma code and the conkers with audiences as emblematic stories to demonstrate teachers' wish to break free from the restrictions imposed on them. In response, teachers are often keen to tell me about their own moments of inspiration and success. Two of these follow, both submitted as written testimony following a session at a young teachers' conference.

Amy is a newly qualified teacher of English in a very challenging school. Her timetable is made up of 'mainly bottom sets, most of whom are boys'. She admits, as any of us who have been there will recognize, that her 'Year 9 classes have (often) descended into vague chaos' with boys 'making comments or raising issues about things that are usually unrelated to the lesson'. Charged with teaching parts of *Great Expectations*, one of her pupils offers a brief literary insight into the character of Miss Havisham as 'a psycho bitch who needs to get laid'. The comment leads to a lively exchange about women's sexual rights, drifting into contemporary perceptions of sexual behaviour. Amy is uncertain about how to proceed. 'I had a spilt-second thought of "oh God, do I let them run with this or do I try and pull it back?"' She trusts herself (and her students) and a relatively orderly, sensible discussion ensues. 'We ended up having a very exciting conversation about the issue of consent and how sex is seen in society. It definitely wasn't anywhere near my lesson plan, but it was definitely one of those hours where I thought they had really gained a lot from what we talked about.'

In the same batch of responses comes Arthur's tale of preparing and carrying out his session on the trial and execution of Anne Boleyn with his Year 6 class. Arthur explains that he teaches in a school in East Anglia with '99 point something per cent EAL' (English as an Additional Language). The six wives of Henry VIII are not part of the cultural heritage of most of his pupils or their families. He is determined that his treatment of the topic will have an impact and so spends hours preparing the session in great detail. I leave Arthur to describe the episode:

> So I got to work making an outrageous (completely historically inaccurate) costume and drinking copious amounts of tea, then using the bags to stain the torn and burnt paper I would hand out with each group's task explained. Then drying each one on the radiator while I watched calligraphy videos on YouTube to ensure my handwriting could pass as 'from the olden days' while remaining accessible to the children. I rehearsed my character (in costume) in front of the mirror at length and tied each piece of paper into a neat scroll with royal red ribbons. I went to bed exhausted, but satisfied and ready to wow my class the next morning.
>
> The lesson was a success. Children who I hadn't reached yet shone and performed rallying speeches of why Anne Boleyn was a victim of mistaken identity. And despite how tired I was, I stayed in character, my hat only fell off twice and I re-enacted beheadings with the same enthusiasm as I had done in the mirror the night before, literally five hours earlier. The hard work had paid off. And the hard work was part of the fun and the only reason it had been a success. I did not moan about how long I had spent doing it because IT WAS WORTH IT! It was a worthwhile activity and created an engaging learning experience where all could be involved and all could achieve in some way (even if that was just to hold up a sign and boo or cheer in the right places). I could see the smiling faces and the passion in the children and feel my hard work actually working, there in front of me.

Incidentally, Arthur's observation that he has no problem with spending time preparing lessons is echoed by many respondents. He goes on to voice an equally common complaint by teachers: he would love to put this sort of effort into preparation, even though he recognizes that this particular instance was somewhat special. The demands of his school's accountability system make this very difficult for him to do:

> Not that my school has a policy against engaging teaching. But I literally do not have the time or energy after marking to a policy that tells me if I give verbal feedback I have to write a little 'V' followed by everything I said, or the planning of each and every lesson in detail with reference to each Assessment Focus which relates to a level which no longer even exists.

Like much testimony gathered from teachers, Arthur's comments frequently refer to his 'passion' for teaching; he epitomizes many of his colleagues' feelings when he talks of his energy being 'wasted on exercises that I cannot feel passionate about because, ultimately, they are 100 per cent useless'.

Tale 5: Belinda tells them to hold on to a thought

In her interview, newly qualified secondary teacher Belinda explains that, as with so many who come to the profession, it was an inspirational teacher of her own who helped her to make her career choice. I ask her if she believes that she could be that inspirational teacher and she replies that she hopes, eventually, to be so. She talks to me of the learning walk, the constant observation and of meetings dominated by graphs, numbers and grade profiles. And then she tells me about an inspirational moment.

The meticulous timing that is supposed to guide her lesson plan has gone awry (as ever) and she approaches the end of the Year 7 lesson without covering everything she should have. Much of this was down to a lively engagement with the topic. Belinda explains that she decides to take a chance with these younger pupils and tells them to take their thought, cup it safely in their hands and bring it to her next lesson. She's not sure if they will comply, but to her delight they play along. She tells me with obvious pleasure how, over the next couple of days, she passes children in the corridor who proudly hold their cupped hands to her and how they do, indeed, bring that thought safely to her next lesson.

There is, as there has been with most of the tales thus far, a moment of bathos. She wants to share this success with colleagues at her next department meeting. 'But meetings aren't about that. They're about data, levels, closing the gap, interventions.' Nonetheless, Belinda remains undeterred and still sees teaching as providing children with 'a doorway to improvement and opportunity'.

Tale 6. Two levels of progress or the miraculous escape of the Chilean miners?

Maurice is a primary school teacher whose responses are characterized by a growing frustration with what he sees as a narrow and restrictive approach to teaching and learning. In common with many of his colleagues, he believes that those charged with managing the process in his school have reduced learning to a series of measurable outcomes, which means that managers have to be furnished with constant proof of 'progress' at every turn. Maurice decides to dig his heels in.

In the autumn of 2010 the uplifting story of the escape of the Chilean miners who were trapped underground for 33 days captured the public imagination (see BBC, 2010). Maurice senses the interest in his Year 5 class and relates how he has to convince a senior manager in the school to alter a scheduled set of sessions designed to generate a required assessment exercise. His persistence pays off and he abandons the schedule to talk to the class and, eventually, get them to write about the miners. His own enthusiasm is captured in this rather breathless and occasionally muddled transcript from his interview:

> What did it feel like for the relatives up there, for them to live life every single day, knowing that they may not see their sons or their daughters or their wives again? We did a piece of writing about the miners underground, how they were feeling, knowing that they may not come up alive. I did another piece of work, subsequently, when the miners came out alive, how the sons or daughter ... a few minutes after they'd found the miner, how they were feeling, using power adverbs, using everything I normally teach with, using all the punctuation, but using something they were inspired by.

In both the interviews I conduct with him, Maurice talks about the way in which the constant requirement to demonstrate 'two levels of progress' has become a dominant mantra at his school. He observes to me that the Chilean miners' episode has been something of a turning-point in terms of how he now views some aspects of teaching: 'I know pupils need to move forward. So I'll do what I think is best to inspire them. I will teach a topic the way I want to do it, and I will be telling people what I think is best, and if Ofsted come in, I will say: this is what works for my pupils – and with confidence.'

Tale 7: Charles and Vernon change the world over a late-night drink

Charles and Vernon, secondary teachers of history and modern languages respectively, tell me about an idea hatched one night on a Year 7 trip to France. The visit has been planned to take pupils to the Bayeux tapestry and, by contrast, the D-Day landings museum at Arromanches. They both point out that their conversation about teaching, over a late night drink, is a rare opportunity to speak about education in this way, echoing earlier comments from respondents about the lack of any kind of space to do this. Vernon reports that 'during the course of a conversation, which we would never have had the time to have during a normal teaching week, we agreed that it would be a good idea if I taught a couple of Year 12 lessons on the French and German political systems to Charles' history classes'. Vernon agrees to introduce some aspects of language to the politics class. As the conversation develops, they agree to go ahead with the project.

The exercise is successful, receiving positive feedback from students even though this is 'not normally something provided for in the syllabuses'. Students are entertained, and impressed that the knowledge of their subject teachers extends beyond that revealed routinely in their classes. Some start to make the connections between language, culture, politics and history, beginning an understanding that goes well beyond examination requirements. The teachers themselves revel in being challenged to take on the unfamiliar. In comments that resonate throughout these ten tales, they are not all concerned about the extra work and preparation this may entail. Vernon's final reflection is illuminating:

> I believe it added an extra dimension to their learning, which would not have happened but for a conversation between two colleagues in two different departments, which would never have happened in the normal hothouse of school.

The tale demonstrates what good teachers know: rather than have meetings between colleagues dominated by data and outcomes, there must be the opportunity to simply discuss ideas and plans – and to use the expertise, knowledge and enthusiasm of each other to develop these even more ambitiously.

Tales 8 and 9. Martin and Vera maintain the great tradition

The literary critic F.R. Leavis, author of *The Great Tradition*, is now considered rather unfashionable in university literature departments. All the same, his famous dictum that 'literature is the supreme means by which you renew your sensuous and emotional life and learn a new awareness' holds sway with a good many English teachers as well as huge numbers of the reading public (Leavis, 1948). It is, however, difficult to imagine what Leavis, or any critic from whatever tradition, might make of the way in which much literature teaching is currently approached in English schools. The fragmentation of texts and their reduction to their component parts is a common complaint from many teachers (see Rosen, 2015, for brilliantly funny comment on this).

Secondary teachers Martin and Vera refuse to play ball. Vera, a teacher with fifteen years' experience, writes of her frustration at having to take 'a great work of literature and reducing the teaching focus to a few pages or a couple of key scenes'. She decides to embark on 'the now outdated and frowned upon idea' of trying to teach the text as a whole. She readily admits that 'tackling 'dense and difficult language' with a 'not especially gifted set 1' in Year 11 'did prove problematic at times'. However, after accepting the challenge, students 'achieved on or above their target grades' and Vera acknowledges the importance of this. For her, however, there is a greater achievement:

> The thing I am most proud of is that one day, whether it be in a university lecture, on a building site or in a pub, if anyone happens to mention *Macbeth* or *Wuthering Heights*, I know that there are at least thirty-one people of a certain age who can say, 'Oh, I've read that. All of it.'

Martin, too, will not settle for diluted versions of the real thing. He is charged with analysing Robert Frost's poem, *Mending Wall* in which the poet challenges the lazy truism that 'good fences make good neighbours'. Martin eschews the approach that 'analyses' the use of metaphors, counts the number of similes or identifies the rhyme scheme; he wants to examine the concept of the effectiveness of walls. He shows video clips of the 'peace walls' in Jerusalem and Belfast – the class is appalled at the former and incredulous at the existence of the latter in the UK. They look at footage of the collapse of the Berlin wall and Martin tells them how red deer, previously conditioned to avoid the electrified border with Czechoslovakia, still refuse to cross, despite the removal of the fence. Do good fences make good neighbours? The class debates the idea with vigour. Martin has struck teaching gold and, what is more, the students understand what the poem is about. By way of contrast with Belinda, who was unable to share her 'cupped hands' idea, Martin is able to talk to colleagues, who happily borrow from these original ideas. Nonetheless, his school's expectations are such that even as the conversation in class flows, he is obliged to truncate it so that pupils write something in their books 'to show' as he wryly observes, 'that we've done some work'.

Tale 10. Abigail lets the hosepipe loose

I leave the final story to Abigail. Recently retired as a primary teacher, her written testimony identifies all of the detrimental features of the GERM and its effect on colleagues and children. She remains, however, unrelentingly optimistic, saying of many young teachers that 'in spite of the bland, prescriptive diet of schemes and plans they were expected to follow, they still worked hard to inspire their pupils'.

In contextualizing a compelling anecdote, she explains that she spends some considerable time happily setting up a session in the school garden and invites a colleague – Mrs B – to join her. The latter, however, is not convinced of the value of the exercise, leaving Abigail a little disappointed and frustrated. Abigail's written response speaks for itself:

> Anyway, to get back to that hot June afternoon. I went to Mrs B's classroom to collect an EAL (children for whom English is an additional language) group I was supporting that afternoon and suggested we take all the children out to work on the garden, and she said she was far too busy in the classroom and would join us later. I gathered up my little group of multilingual gardeners and we left the rest to do the 'real learning' in the hot stuffy classroom. We spent a long time tending to our plot of vegetables and herbs, writing labels, looking for changes, enjoying the textures and smells, discovering insects and all the other experiences you would expect and then decided our plants needed a drink so out came the hose pipe. We gave the beds a good watering and by this time Mrs B had joined us with the rest of the class. When one of my newly arrived Polish boys saw her, he called out 'Mrs B it wet'. Naturally I took this to mean he wanted me to point the hosepipe at Mrs B and soak her to the skin. She had particularly annoyed me that afternoon so I did just that. The noise and hysteria that followed generated a large audience of pupils and staff including the Head and Deputy.

Mrs B, the teaching assistant (TA), 30 small people and myself were completely drenched. Fortunately Mrs B and her TA saw the funny side and of course the children loved it. The hosepipe moment had not been in my lesson plan, I had not done a risk assessment and several nearby lessons had been disturbed but somehow I was forgiven. As for my little Polish boy, the next day he drew a beautiful detailed picture of the garden and wrote his first ever sentence in English: 'I wet in gdn.' I was very proud and so was his mum.

Abigail concludes her written commentary with a personal note to me, which could also serve as an accurate epigram for this book. She writes, 'I think what I'm trying to say is that many teachers have their hosepipe moments and many dare to open cans of worms (a reference to an earlier part of her testimony) when the time seems right. God bless 'em all.'

These ten uplifting tales are just a selection from a whole range of possible stories. In the course of interviewing teachers and eliciting written testimony from them, I found their great enthusiasm for sharing such moments to be the most gratifying and enjoyable feature of the research. Teachers wanted to share such moments because they mean something to them and their students. The view that *this* is what they came into teaching for is expressed in various ways when such tales are told. I hope the teachers reading them will recognize much of their own practice, and that others – be they parents, students or teacher educators – recall such moments from their own school experience.

It is also important to understand that in following their instincts in this way, teachers, knowingly or not, are acknowledging what classic educational theorists and commentators have been writing about for decades. The removal of pedagogical studies from the training of most teachers, much less any consideration of notions such as child psychology or development, has often been a hindrance to teachers being genuinely reflective about their practice in an informed way. Yet the most cursory of whistle-stop tours through the work of writers on pedagogy would convince these beheaders of Anne Boleyn and cuppers of ideas that they are, indeed, really doing the right thing.

Jerome Bruner, writing in 1960, pointed to the fact that 'interest in the material to be learned is the best stimulus to learning, rather than such external goals as grades or later competitive advantage' (Bruner, 1960: 14). Bruner went on to observe that 'motives for learning must be kept from going passive ... they must be based as much as possible upon the arousal of interest in what there is to be learned' (80). In his classic work from over fifty years ago about how children in the education system learn, or sometimes fail to learn, John Holt writes that:

> The human mind … is a mystery and, in large part, will probably always be so. It takes even the most thoughtful, honest and introspective person many years to learn even a small part of what goes on in his own mind. How, then, can we be sure about what goes on in the mind of another? Yet many people talk as if we could measure and list the contents of another person's mind as easily, accurately and fully as the contents of a suitcase.
>
> (Holt, 1991: xv)

When Vygotsky expresses the idea that 'human learning presupposes a specific social nature and a process by which children grow into the intellectual life of those around them' (Vygotsky, 1978: 88), he is pointing to the fact that the process of learning cannot be what Freire (1990) describes as an act of 'depositing' knowledge, in a way that ignores humanity and human behaviour. Teachers know this well, whether or not they are aware of the work of such theorists.

Holly, a teacher of physical education in a secondary school, tells me a story about depositing that makes this former teacher of English smile. She was attending a meeting of heads of department in her school where the leadership team of the school plans for ways in which they can improve the scores in its overall results' profile. In a peculiar parlour game, certain subjects are assigned values and are allocated to particular 'buckets'. I check that I have heard her correctly. Yes, buckets. Her PE bucket is low value. English, Mathematics and Science are high value. A conversation ensues in the meeting about ways to ensure how the high value buckets are to be filled. I have a final check to make certain she is not pulling my leg.

I hope that I have never been, and never become, one of those grumpy old teachers who harrumphs about the perceived ignorance of younger generations. Not everyone will be familiar with the works of Irish poet W.B. Yeats or the novels of Dickens. Holly's senior team clearly was not. Yeats wrote that 'education is not the filling of a pail but the lighting of a fire'. In his picture of the Victorian schoolroom at the start of *Hard Times*, Dickens has Thomas Gradgrind – 'what I want is Facts. Teach these boys and girls nothing but Facts. Facts alone are wanted in life' – survey the class to see 'little vessels then and there arranged in order, ready to have imperial gallons of facts poured into them until they were full to the brim'. Whether or not Holly's colleagues had read Dickens, Bruner or Vygotsky, their practice is as perfect an illustration of 'depositing' as we could have. Fortunately, as testimony in this chapter demonstrates, teachers still prefer fire-lighting to bucket-filling.

One final idea needs to be addressed here. The stories and episodes referred to above confirm, as the title of this book suggests, that the spirit of teachers has not been crushed. Every parent, child and member of the public should be encouraged by this: inspiring, creative teachers are what we all want. There is, however, one constituency within the profession that sometimes needs reminding of the energy and inventiveness that still characterizes the actions of many teachers – and that is their more experienced colleagues.

From my conversations with them it appears that a significant number of older teachers – by no means all – subscribe to the idea that the self-disciplining of the profession through the accountability agenda is now immovably entrenched. This is captured in the observation of one such experienced respondent in the original set of interviews conducted in 2012. Shaun, highly experienced, identifies what he sees as a generation of teachers who are happy to use pre-planned resources and to 'teach to that' and 'want to be told what to do'. In December 2011, I decided to put this to the test.

I contacted 13 teachers with whom I was professionally acquainted, each of whom had a minimum of fifteen years' experience. I explained that the purpose of my approach was to test my perception that experienced colleagues often held the view that few new entrants to the profession were willing to challenge the status quo. Respondents were asked to indicate their response to the notion that in the last five to ten years, teachers new to the profession were prepared to challenge what I then called 'the accountability agenda'. Within days of the start of the Christmas break I had received responses from twelve of them. All bar one indicated that they felt that new entrants had bought into the current agenda and this differing response was qualified by a note explaining that any challenge would only happen 'if they were any good'. In the view of this small and somewhat random cohort, who had been captured in something of a snapshot, it became clear that the perception of acquiescence was strong.

The lengthy written testimony, provided voluntarily by many of this particular cohort, was especially illuminating. One respondent observed: 'it's a good question, because I could go on about this at length – and on the second day of my holiday too!' The comments themselves are heartfelt and passionate. One teacher despairs of the 'Orwellian trance of compliance' she observes around her, while another bemoans the 'general gobbledegook of pseudo-management speak that has permeated our profession' and sees 'very little challenge to it from the new generation'. Such sentiments are common. They are summarized by a primary school headteacher of some twenty years who observes that 'it is all they have known so they don't imagine it can be different'.

I mention this research to reinforce a couple of ideas referred to earlier. In a working life where team meetings are limited to progress checks and data trawls, there is little space for teachers to actually communicate thoughts and ideas about their beliefs, actions and even their abilities. And in a working environment that has closed down the metaphorical and literal spaces for such discussion – the loss of staffrooms, lunch-hours spent in frenetic activity – the opportunity for informal, professional conversation is lost. In the whirligig of activity which is often confused with 'ensuring progress' or 'raising standards' the outmoded idea of genuine professional dialogue falls by the wayside and we end up in a position where even those with an apparently common interest fail to see and appreciate each other's abilities. When applied to the labour process the term 'alienation' is laden with a variety of interpretations and analyses, but common to any such understanding of the term is the way in which prevalent material conditions can affect social relationships. One of the effects of the marketization of education is the diminution of collective conversation, and the easy exchange of ideas that could and should work to the benefit of students and teachers alike. Those who suspect that newer entrants to the profession have empty spirits would do well to find the time to test that proposition more closely.

In describing the features of the GERM, Sahlberg identifies principal contributors to the infection as: low-risk ways to reach learning goals, a focus on core subjects and a standardization of education. In the selected anecdotes that form the basis of this chapter, all three of these elements are present – and all three are, to some extent, resisted by teachers. The chapter that follows looks at the way in which some of those charged with leading schools are also in sympathy with the fire-lighters that Yeats wanted educators to be.

Chapter 7

Can school leaders let the caged bird sing?

The previous chapter demonstrated how teachers remain determined to keep the spark alive – and know how to do so. In all the evidence gathered since 2010, teachers talk of the way in which, despite obstructions placed in their way, they feel largely trusted in their own schools – always depending, of course, on the 'delivery' of the right results. They say how they often feel supported by a management in whom they, broadly speaking, have confidence. It would not be accurate to say that this state of affairs is enjoyed by all my respondents, but primary teacher Melissa captures the flavour of much of what is said when she talks in a carefully qualified way of being trusted 'in this school, to a certain extent'. The institution itself and its leaders have enormous influence on how autonomously teachers can behave and, as a consequence, the confidence they feel about following their more creative instincts.

The role of the headteacher in 2015 is unrecognizable from what it was in the past. It may not be true to say that every beginning teacher once carried the field marshal's baton in her or his knapsack – although many chose to avoid this, it is fair to say that an aspiration to school leadership was a feature of many teachers' careers. However, the high-stakes, high-pressure world of a marketized system has led us to the point where headships can now be searched for on social media as head-hunting firms seek suitable candidates for posts that are deemed unattractive and untenably onerous (Selvarajah, 2015). What is indisputable is that a headteacher's actions now have huge influence on the way a school manages its affairs, successfully or otherwise (see, for example, National College for Leadership of Schools, 2010).

Many respondents chose to discuss the actions of school leaders in their comments and writing and, while they acknowledged that these leaders were not malevolent, they often expressed disappointment with their conduct. Clarke's comments provide a fair synthesis of such observations:

> I understand that these features of our school are not necessarily because our leadership are malicious individuals, rather they are
> … under pressure from our current twisted education system,

itself gripped by a psychotic accountability agenda for teachers. What I do hold against our leadership, however, is their lack of solidarity with fellow educators. For all our head's flaws, he was a teacher once.

Clarke articulates a common view: the people who enforce the worst aspect of GERM are not bad, mean or stupid. Rather, he sees them – in most cases, at least – as fellow professionals constrained to act in ways that, in their heart of hearts, they know to be faintly absurd. Educational sociologist Basil Bernstein captured this perfectly when describing the 'dislocation between the culture of pedagogic discourse [whereby teachers seek to do what *they* feel is essentially "right" for their students] and a management ethos which has become the device for creating an entrepreneurial competitive culture' (Bernstein, 1996: 75). A headteacher in Stephen Ball's 2013 study on teacher resistance talks of attempting to repel 'the audit-managerial monolith' (Ball and Olmedo, 2013: 91) that exhausts the teachers in his school. Music teacher Laura bemoans the way in which respected colleagues take part in such auditing and when I ask her whether she thinks they believe in it all, looks at me rather witheringly and exclaims, 'of course not!'

Responses from some senior figures themselves indicate how they pride themselves on protecting teachers from the worst excesses of what is often termed 'initiative overload'. Others are unapologetic about ensuring that the school's public profile remains healthy, thereby protecting the jobs and salaries of the teachers. Despite this, the first part of this chapter looks at the mismatch that exists between what school leaders profess and how their actions are interpreted by teachers. Later evidence provides some heartening illustrations of ways that leaders can create the circumstances for GERM resistance.

Having conducted research into their professional autonomy with teachers in 2010–11, I decided that I needed to put the findings from this to some headteachers and school leaders in 2011–12. Most of their comments are at some variance with the views of classroom teachers. Headteacher Bernadette is adamant that she tells teachers 'don't stick to ... the bog standard. Raise your game. Do something a bit different. And I've said that every September training day. This is your year to do something a bit outside the box.' Albert and Charles, both headteachers of very successful schools, identify a different problem: Albert expresses ire at teachers and their 'angst' about their own professional autonomy when 'they are much freer than they think they are'. Charles makes the point that some teachers are overanxious: 'some of my staff wouldn't think they are free'. Such comments typify much of what emerges from our conversations: despite experiencing the pressure to perform in their own capacity as school leaders, they appear strangely oblivious to the similar demands being encountered by their own teachers. This may be a touch unfair to headteachers as a whole; this was a small sample and, as we shall see later, there are other examples of Heads who take a much more enlightened approach. Nonetheless, there appears to be a mismatch between what senior figures are saying and what the foot-soldiers are experiencing.

One other factor emerges from the conversation with leaders: to put it crudely, that there is one law for the rich and one for the poor. David, a headteachers' representative puts it like this:

> I think we've got a real polarization within our school system at the moment. We've got some schools which are almost immune ... whatever they do. Then there are other schools which are much more vulnerable ... and those schools have to jump through every hoop when some new initiative comes out.

In many respects, this is precisely what government policy is designed to encourage. As far back as 1997, Labour education secretary David Blunkett established the principle that 'where schools are evidently successful, we see no benefit in interfering with their work, although all schools need to be challenged to improve' (Secretary of State for Education, 1997: 12). This is reflected in much current testimony from Heads and teachers and indicates that there is an inequality built into the very structure of the inspection system. Headteacher Bernadette begins her interview by telling me that in all her years as Head, she has 'never felt so powerless, overwhelmed, pressurized and stressed'. Her school achieves average success in terms of exam passes, but compares poorly with other schools that have significant intake from more advantaged households. Bernadette becomes visibly frustrated as she describes how she would like to break free from what she sees as ill-considered requirements from Ofsted, but goes on to ask herself:

> But am I brave enough to say, these are our children; these are our stakeholders, this is how we're going to carry on? No, because actually the impact of that would be ... and I know this, it would be falling rolls which would then lead to difficulties ... and I'm not prepared to do that to staff or the existing children.

Secondary teacher Leanne moved from a school in very challenging circumstances to one in a more favoured area during the course of her two interviews with me. When reflecting on a fierce regime of inspection and scrutiny at the original school, she talks of how the prospect of not reaching target grades would mean that 'we'll be looked at and we'll have to refine our practices, but [teachers felt] absolute terror ... that's probably a strong word, but that's the way it felt'. When pushed on whether 'terror' is, perhaps, hyperbolic, she concedes that 'panic may be better. There was always an underlying sense of panic.' I ask her if she would ever consider moving back to a more challenging environment and she replies that she could not. 'I couldn't go back to a school that was under so much pressure.' The responses of the teachers are littered with tales of imposed uniformity of approach and crudely applied performance checks – and these are particularly acute in schools that are not well favoured in terms of inspection outcomes. This is borne out in Hutchings' 2015 study which reveals that 'teachers in schools with the most disadvantaged pupils, those with below average attainment and those with the lowest Ofsted ratings reported use of these strategies significantly more than teachers in other schools' (Hutchings, 2015: 24).

There is little doubt that any such accusations of inequality of treatment would be met with vigorous denial from politicians charged with running the system and the Heads who have to do their bidding, but there may be gaps in perception here. Sometimes – perhaps frequently – it is difficult for hard-working classroom teachers to take the announcements of their political leaders seriously. For example, Ofsted and its paymasters in government know that they have to pay a degree of lip-service towards acknowledging that some schools start with an inbuilt advantage. The link between social disadvantage and educational achievement is now universally acknowledged (OECD, 2012). Recognizing this, schools that are 'coasting' are, we are told, to be subjected to inspection as well as those that are demonstrably 'underperforming'. Most recently, the 2015 Education and Adoption Bill (Parliament, 2015a) brings our notice to this, in the statement that: 'the Secretary of State may by regulations define what "coasting" means in relation to a school' on its second page. Regrettably, no such definition of the term, or anything close to it, appears in the publication. In a further example of the rhetoric of government not filtering down to the shop floor, Ofsted's recommendations that teachers should not need to constantly recap learning in lessons, should not jump from one activity to another and should not need to refer to learning objectives with tiring frequency (Ofsted, 2012) are much more honoured in the breach than the observance, as the tyranny of the learning walk prevails. David's observations about polarization in the system and the unrelenting demands of measurability and scrutiny, reinforce the central importance of the headteacher. Yet, however well-intentioned that Head may be, she or he still is bound by circumstances that can end up with good intentions paving the way to hell for the classroom teacher, bearing the brunt of a GERM-ridden system.

To return to another of the central tenets of the argument: no one is disputing that the pursuit of the best outcomes for all children is anything other than a completely non-negotiable factor for all schools and all teachers. It is a grotesque distortion of the debate when those who dislike criticism of how schools are run immediately reach for the argument about dissenters being the enemies of promise. It is also true to say that children who start school at a disadvantage should be those on whom attention is concentrated in an attempt to address inequality. The popular argument from the right that 'poverty is no excuse' is a gross over-simplification, but teachers need no lessons on the need for high expectations or about refusing to write off the chances of large swathes of young people. But trying to do the best by such students is not the same as turning schools into exam factories where coaching, rehearsal and rote-learning become the rule rather than the exception. When a Level 3 or a D grade – or whatever that may mean by 2017 (see the Assessment and Qualifications Alliance website, AQA, 2015) – represents failure, irrespective of what such an outcome may represent for the achievement of a particular child, the necessity of engaging in such retrogressive practice becomes inevitable. Whether a student actually learns anything in such circumstances becomes immaterial.

An interview in 2015 with Patrick, the headteacher of a secondary school in challenging circumstances, provides a telling illustration of how this need to chase results plays out. With vast experience and an established local reputation as a headteacher of integrity, I enjoy our conversation together – a conversation in which he turns to the welfare of his students, all his staff, teaching and non-teaching alike, and to the place of his school in a challenging community. He talks to me about fostering talent and ability in his teachers; of the 'wow moments' he sees around the school; of his 'core beliefs of good work, good order and good relationships'. He relates how some of his teachers, far from living in dread of seeing him on a learning walk, tell him that they value his presence and conversations and reflections ensue about what he has seen. He proudly shows me the school's weekly bulletin in which he doesn't shirk from some difficult comments about an incident earlier in the week. It is impossible not to be impressed by his honesty and openness.

I ask him about what I know to have been a difficult previous year for him. The school had experienced a run of poor GCSE results. In an area where other schools enjoy better reputations, his has been at the bottom of the pile in terms of parental choice. I use the phrase 'under the cosh' and he nods knowingly. What is more, he tells me, quoting one of his senior staff, if the GCSE results of 2015 were those by which any final judgement about the future of the school had to be made, this would not be the year 'to bet the farm on it'. Failure could mean being forced into academy status or being coerced into federation with a neighbouring school. I venture to suggest that many schools faced with such drastic circumstances might retreat to formulaic and restricted practices to ensure that the results were obtained. Did his school do so?

He tells me that the school placed significant time and resources into ensuring that this particular Year 11 achieved good results in English and mathematics. There were significant after-school 'interventions'. There were weekend interventions. And interventions during holiday periods. Staff were told that 'this is where we are; this is what we have to do; these are the implications and this is what we owe our community'. He goes on to describe a programme of coaching and preparation that required intense and concentrated effort by the teachers and students alike. The sole aim of this provision was to haul young people over grade boundaries and in these terms it had been successful. I consider it tactless and impolite to press him on whether such an approach was, indeed, formulaic. What had been put in place in the school was a necessary survival mechanism. Young people had their grades, the school lived to fight another day, jobs had been made secure and self-esteem had been bolstered all round. By any measure it would be unconscionably churlish not to recognize this as a massive achievement.

Nevertheless, the question for educators persists: does this combination of performativity and survivalism correspond to any credible conception of what education is and what it is for? Is the production of human capital in a competitive world such a hegemonic demand that the production of outcomes – however welcome – justifies a regime of coaching and rehearsal in the name of improving standards? And what if those standards, attained through such concerted activity on the part of teacher and learner, do not measure up to the requirements of those captains of industry whose ambitions teachers seem to have requisitioned and who voice 'concern over the job-readiness of too many young people' (CBI, 2014: 5)?

Notwithstanding the humanity and open-mindedness of some Heads, it remains difficult for teachers to hold on to an enduring idea of something better to offer children – but they do so all the same. We have seen that teachers carry within themselves a strong conception of what good teaching and learning look like. It is worth reiterating that the examples given in the previous chapter are but a selection from a range of tales that could have filled a separate volume. As well as making individual efforts, which occasionally have to verge on the clandestine, there are still some teachers who are supported by school leaders whose actions bear out their rhetoric of freedom, autonomy and an adherence to pedagogic principles. What follows is an illustration of what can happen when it is these qualities, rather than the requirements of the GERM, which determine the actions of educators.

Professional conversations and connections take me to two primary schools where I am led to believe that a more relaxed regime than normal operates. However, for this part of my research I wanted, as always, to talk to teachers rather than school leaders in the first instance. Only after my meetings with teachers did I pursue the theme of autonomy and freedom with the headteachers of these schools. Their comments appear below. But first, it is the views and the voices of the teachers that are relevant. Although it's a rather sentimental trope, I call the two schools Grace and Hope. Grace is a bustling school in inner London, its intake reflecting the socially and ethnically mixed nature of the neighbourhood. Hope is located in a market town in the east of England, and also reflects its mixed socio-economic location, although it is less ethnically diverse. I meet a self-selecting group of the teachers from each of the schools at separate times in the summer of 2015. We share after-school tea and biscuits, I switch on the recorder and they talk. I am, for the most part, an appreciative silent witness.

It is important not to overstate the point here, but these schools are, indeed, different from many of those in which my respondents work inasmuch as they can be characterized as liberal and open-minded in the way they are run. A Hope teacher talks of the 'relaxed' ethos of the school, saying it is commented on by parents and visitors and is a feature of relationships between teacher and pupils as well. At Grace they talk of being valued by their school leaders and of being encouraged to try different approaches and methods. Nevertheless, it would be dishonest to characterize either school as a haven from the storm of data, results and measurability that besets their colleagues elsewhere. The usual complaints surface with regularity. At Grace, with absolutely no prompting from me, teachers lead the conversation and spend the first eight minutes berating Ofsted, the government and the media view of teachers. Hope teachers echo this: 'suddenly, to be average is to be terrible' complains one; 'politicians have absolutely no idea about what we do and how children learn' says another.

If they are united with many of their colleagues in their negative views of aspects of their professional life, the teachers at these schools also articulate much that is positive that has been said in other interviews. They are not afraid of hard work as long as it is for the benefit of children. Preparation and worthwhile assessment are embraced as necessary and central to their practice. They are prepared for it 'to be tough at times' and accept that there are parts of the job that can be tiresome. They 'want to do things properly and make a difference' and, in the words of a Grace teacher, 'we're not trying to get out of work and we're not trying to dodge anything'. They want to raise standards – although they don't believe that testing is the way to do this: a Grace teacher entertains us by pointing out that 'they want us to differentiate in 70,000 different ways, taking into account each child's needs ... then they give them all the same test at the same time!' They know that they need to be accountable and, as expressed by another Grace teacher, believe that they understand this better than their political masters who 'write off' some children because of grades and test results. In their positivity and determination their approaches are identical to those of their peers elsewhere.

What marks the experience of these teachers out as different is their view of the way in which their respective schools are organized and run. Again, it is important not to make unsubstantiated claims: I am not suggesting that there are no other schools that are thoughtful and liberal in their approach and none of this is to cast as villains those headteachers who, as we have seen, believe that they do allow autonomy and freedom, even if that isn't how it's seen in the classroom. Hope teachers express their deep-seated belief that 'this really is a child-centred school' which draws a clear distinction between learning and the curriculum. They know that failure and mistakes are tolerated, even encouraged, for both staff and children, as part of the learning process. One talks of an occasion when she 'really messed up and so just went in to [the Head] and told her I'd done the wrong thing'. The Head does not let her off lightly, but the teacher herself makes the point that she was confident enough to admit to her mistake 'and would do so again'. Grace teachers talk proudly about how, in the test-driven, high-stakes environment of Year 6, 'we still do stuff like the brass band and lots of topic work'. The conversations of both sets of teachers are full of laughter and in-jokes about the failed aeroplane experiment in the playground or being on the carpet with the class convulsed by giggles.

Both sets of teachers are unequivocal in their beliefs that their difference from most schools stems from the values and principles of their headteachers. Some talk of having come from elsewhere where school life is much more tightly controlled; one relates how he refused promotion elsewhere because of what he saw as a small-minded, oppressive view of education; another, who has some significant experience, says that if the current Head leaves, she will too. They talk of being trusted and, above all, of knowing that a set of principles beyond what a Hope teacher calls 'the robotic approach that the government wants' informs their leaders' actions.

Before we explore where this confident liberalism on the part of their leaders comes from, a final point must be made about my meetings with the teachers. First, the meetings were set up with the full consent and total support of the headteachers. Both gatherings were in comfortable surroundings on school property. Conscious of the fact that I was using their time at the end of busy school days, I tried on both occasions to bring the conversation to a close at what I deemed to be a suitable point. It proved quite difficult to do. Given the opportunity to talk about education, its purpose, children and their approach to teaching, the teachers relished the chance to do so. Both sets of teachers ended the meetings by thanking *me* for giving them the time and space to do so! Earlier sections of this book have dealt with the closing down of spaces for teachers to discuss their practice and their experience. Readers may be left to draw conclusions about the fact that in schools that are successfully led, by those who trust their teachers, such discourse is openly encouraged.

I arrange to meet the headteachers of Hope and Grace, Jessica and Sam respectively, to try to discern what they bring to their post that inspires their teachers' evident loyalty and respect. Unsurprisingly, much of it stems from a political perspective, personal belief and experience. Both heads have been committed teacher trade unionists throughout their working lives. Jessica talks about how her actions are informed by what she has learnt – good and bad – from the headteachers under whom she has worked. Both readily reveal that they were not academic high-flyers and Jessica cites instances when she has to persuade school governors to appoint teachers whose qualities she considers to be good for her school but who, similarly, do not have glittering exam results. It is when they talk about the level of commitment, accountability and sense of moral purpose – a concept with which they are both very comfortable – that I begin to form a greater sense of what is at the bottom of their professional conduct and the positive impact it has on the teachers with whom they work.

They talk of absolute rigour, but a light touch when it comes to checking planning and marking. They speak of trust: Sam says that he always looks for teachers 'having the same intentions for kids as I do' and Jessica advocates 'reminding ourselves about why we came into education'. Sam uses the phrase 'pedagogic responsibility' when explaining what he wants from teachers, and both Heads recognize that what Jessica characterizes as 'fear and coercion' will not bring out the best in people as much as genuine trust. Both are deeply resentful of what they see as the attitude of recent governments towards schools and teachers. Sam is particularly irked:

> Those in charge of education don't get us. They assume we're teachers because we're work-shy. Why didn't we become merchant bankers? Because we're not good enough! But we don't need to be given deadlines, thresholds and targets because we're already working our bloody socks off.

They both express disappointment with some fellow Heads who they see as data-driven, overly ambitious for personal recognition and 'all about the shine and polish'. Having been Head of a school in difficult circumstances, Jessica is confident that it is not necessary to sacrifice creativity and intelligence in order to meet standards and get results – 'you can have both' – but she appreciates that 'a climate of fear' can quickly take hold in schools. It is then up to the headteacher to set the 'moral compass', ensuring that a balance is struck and that, as Sam points out, 'kids don't just do dance and basket-weaving because it's fun and everyone has a nice time. We learn to read and write – that's non-negotiable'. In my conversations with them, their sense of responsibility to their teachers, their children and the communities they serve surfaces regularly, as does their willingness to work hard and be accountable to a range of people. 'We don't try to wriggle out of things' explains Sam: it is an honesty and openness that plays well with their teachers.

I give the final anecdote to Max, a headteacher who made sure that formerly caged birds did, indeed, sing. I first interviewed him in 2010. Max's school was earmarked for closure in 2012 as part of a local authority restructuring. The school had not been identified as being in any way deficient in performance and was in no worse a state of physical disrepair than others in the area. Examination results were comparable with similar schools and the school itself enjoyed a good reputation in the town. The closure announcement was seen by the teachers as both unfair and arbitrary. As student numbers diminished, Max and senior leaders began to see opportunities in this adversity, enhanced, as he readily recognized, by a spirit of bloody-mindedness born of their perceived unfair treatment. He decided to invest in 'morale, into giving teachers the autonomy, the empowering of people and the whole thing'.

Above all, staff were strongly encouraged to 'do what we think is right'. In a revealing passage Max talked of the unexpected benefit of facing closure, describing a situation where the relaxation of the usual paraphernalia of control and auditability is a precursor to greater autonomy:

It is weird, it is perverse, it's very strange. But suddenly, because we're closing, a whole black cloud ... and the black cloud would be pressures ... the pressures, the professional pressures we were under, suddenly a black cloud has been lifted in a sense, in that we can take more risks, and in that we can have ... professionals can take ... more chances, you know, more scope, because, OK, the big pressure is the standards one, the big stick is Ofsted, and that's been taken away.

In a telling development, national exam results in the school improved and Max is unequivocal in drawing a correspondence between such improvement and the lifting of the 'black cloud'.

When I interview him again in 2015 I want to check that he still feels the same about the situation as he did five years ago. He remains visibly enthusiastic and stands by all he said. He talks of 'buoyancy' and 'the best opportunity to produce the sort of education we wanted'. He considers the episode to have given a 'message about results, staff morale, pupil morale, overall well-being and a great learning environment'. In a commentary about what he considers to have been the best of what he saw – and still sees – about teachers bringing energy and vitality to classrooms despite forces ranged against them, he spontaneously coins the phrase 'the indomitable spirit of a teacher who can turn a bland moment into an opportunity'. I tell him that I may yet consider using this wonderful observation as a perfect strapline for this book – and it is, indeed, the strapline for Chapter 3.

Extrapolation and generalization from the sort of qualitative evidence we have here – conversations with heads and teachers – is fraught with difficulty (Firestone, 1993). The original research did not set out to examine the psyches of headteachers and school leaders and neither did the gathering of testimony from them in 2015. To make a claim that there are particular personal qualities that might promote more liberated attitudes is unrealistic, especially given the fact that material circumstances in which heads operate will almost certainly be just as influential as personal preferences and beliefs. What this chapter has attempted to do is to draw attention to the extent to which leadership might liberate teachers – and to demonstrate that there are some such instances and that this is cause for celebration. We now go on to look at how teachers take to self-activity to do this for themselves.

Chapter 8

Doing it for themselves: How teachers can take greater control of the curriculum

I own up. I was an INSET terrorist. Educational blogger David Didau must have been watching me on the dreaded training days:

> All too often the only requirement for staff is that they sit and listen. Either to an expensive motivational guest speaker or to a member of the school's own leadership team. Teachers tend to be fairly intolerant of this and have a tendency to misbehave. We know that if we took this approach in an observed lesson we'd be (rightly) lambasted so we resent having it inflicted on us. Why does it happen? Cos it's easy. The expensive motivational guest speaker will have delivered his (it's *always* a bloke!) spiel many times before and can just trot out the same old same old and pick up their pay cheque.
>
> (Didau, 2013)

Didau isn't overstating the case. Teacher training days were introduced as part of the educational reforms of the late 1980s. The Conservative government of the time made a flawed attempt at nailing down teachers' hours because of a series of strikes over pay and conditions. These calculations are still entrenched in the annually revised *School Teachers' Pay and Conditions Document*, available online and usually blithely ignored by teachers and their managers, who remain unaware of its existence. Parts of these terms stipulate that teachers should be available for work on 195 days in any year and that 190 of these should be in contact with children. What to do with the remaining 5? The days were soon dubbed Baker Days after the Secretary of State who introduced them – a friend once unkindly suggested that this should be truncated to 'B-days' for a number of reasons that readers can leave to their imagination. Rather than use these days for sensible activities like joint planning or just plain catching-up, school leaders discovered the inspirational speaker and the expert – and the ground for the breeding of the INSET/CPD terrorist was prepared.

In the quarter of a century since the implementation of the 1988 Educational Reform Act, a procession of advisers, experts and consultants have lined up – and lined their pockets – to tell the beleaguered teacher just where she is going wrong and how he (and Didau is right, it's usually a he) has just the thing to put her on the right track. This is not to suggest that there has been no innovative thinking and illuminating comment along the way; it's just that there has been an awful lot of snake-oil sold, beside authentic medicine. In a neoliberal context that opens schools to market forces, we should not be surprised that some disreputable salesmen will seize opportunities for financial gain. This may be in the form of fashioning oneself as an expert in behaviour management or learning styles, promoting systems for reporting and data collection or, on a more nakedly commercial level, pushing particular forms of technology and digital material. With the standardization of education – one of the principal characteristics of the GERM – comes the opportunity for the production of standardized materials and, in its turn, the advocacy of teaching materials in the pursuit of profit, masquerading under the tired old guise of 'spreading good practice'.

I became an INSET terrorist because I could, like Hamlet and tens of thousands of teachers, tell a hawk from a handsaw. This chapter describes a whole range of ways in which undefeated teachers no longer look to the expert and consultant, but to their own devices, their own intellect and their own collective knowledge to get the most from themselves to give to their students. And I do acknowledge that there are some brilliantly inspirational speakers out there who do bring knowledge and expertise to schools – and if you're one of them, you are honourably excluded from some of these comments.

In September 2015 I visit Georgina, who is a senior leader in a large secondary school in outer London. Three years earlier we had met to discuss a bold plan to develop her school's CPD programme. Charged with its oversight, she had become aware that large sums of money were being spent on enjoyable but largely ineffective INSET days – and that the 'terrorists' had been out in force. Nonetheless, it was not so much their presence that concerned her – they were, after all, a distinct minority – it was the temporary, transitory nature of the outcomes from the days themselves that troubled her. 'We'd had a lovely day and we'd had some great ideas, but once this initial glow had worn off and ordinary life kicked in, we hadn't gained much from it.' What Georgina was looking for was something that could be self-sustaining in terms of real professional development, long after the feel-good factor of a day out and lunch in a comfortable hotel had dissipated. We devised a plan whereby the university education department and the school would work in partnership, to establish research groups around a small number of priorities identified by the staff themselves. For a year the school's training budget was subsumed into the project as we worked to establish a culture of self-prompted research and inquiry into practice. Staff, including non-teaching staff, engaged in coaching conversations and discussion groups about teaching and learning. Some embarked on serious reading about pedagogy for the first time since they had qualified; others engaged with structured, formalized research leading in some cases to study at master's level. The objective had been to establish a self-sustaining approach to professional development that would go well beyond what Georgina characterizes as 'rocking and rolling through all the Govian changes'. Has this different approach worked or has it too been just another passing phase?

Georgina is adamant that this has been no flash in the pan. In our conversation she reminds me that the new approach to CPD had been born of weariness with 'being spoken to and having stuff demonstrated'. She acknowledges that some outside speakers had been excellent but that none of the outcomes 'had ever embedded themselves into the school's psyche'. There had been 'no continuing dialogue … nothing to sustain it'. She was not, however, to be defeated: 'it would have been so easy to get grumpy about it and think that teachers are disengaged, but they're not'. The upshot of the project, now continuing largely independently from the university, is the production of what she calls 'a thoughtful school'. She talks about how the idea of research and inquiry now runs through everything they do, about a willingness to take risks and of an environment in which discussion, not 'telling', is the hallmark of school meetings. Expert outsiders are rare and when they do make an intervention it is usually to guide the research actions of the teachers. It is this self-efficacy, sometimes referred to as agency, which is at the centre of much of this chapter and the next. This notion of teacher agency is brilliantly explored by researcher Sarah Robinson who, happily for the central thesis of this book, draws the conclusion that 'the evidence illustrates that, despite the strategies of performance, accountability and control mechanisms … the presence of strong collegial relationships enabled the teachers to construct their professional agency by adaptation and adoption of policy requirements to fit some practices and reshape others' (Robinson, 2012: 231). The work of Georgina and her colleagues takes this notion of agency beyond 'collegial relationships' and into the area of valid, reliable research which sometimes challenges the status quo and the 'what works' agenda (see Alexander, 2004).

In widening the scope of CPD to include research into practice, Georgina and her school are part of a wider movement of genuine enquiry by teachers into their own practice. A quick internet search reveals dozens of such instances and although there remains a stubborn and traditional resistance to this notion from some academics, who appear to consider the encroachment onto their territory by mere artisan practitioners as problematic (Stewart, 2015; Wiliam, 2015), many schools continue to see the way forward as taking inquiry into their own hands rather than deferring to yet more experts. As well as engaging with research, despite the stifling effect of a testing regime that encroaches on all aspects of school life at all times of the year, there is also an appetite among teachers to challenge a rigidly standardized curriculum that suppresses any love of learning. To illustrate this I mention two episodes; one very contemporary and another some ten years old.

The latter concerns the aftermath of the Boxing Day tsunami in 2004. A friend calls to tell me about something he has done. In the first staff briefing of the calendar year, he sits along with his colleagues at the meeting where the usual litany of data and directives are trotted out from senior leaders. As he half listens, he is made aware of another voice in the room that has interrupted proceedings to make an impassioned plea to those assembled there. The voice is his own. (To those of you who think this absurd, I can assure you that it is the very mark of an activist to sit in such meetings, swear to yourself that you won't become irate and impatient or say something imprudent, only to find yourself, as if by unstoppable instinct, on your feet and making the very comment you had pledged to keep to yourself.) My friend points out that parts of the world nearly came to an end; that whole tracts of land have disappeared; families have been torn apart and that in a world characterized by technological advance, no-one had thought to use this knowledge to stop us destroying the planet or, at the very least, deploying technology to install better warning systems. Surely, he says, we should be talking about this with our young people? He resumes his seat expecting the mixture of silent support that often follows his interventions, along with the eyebrow-raising of the more pragmatic or bored. After all, what has any of this to do with raising achievement or the new behaviour-management system? What follows astonishes him.

Voices speak up in support of what he has said. Colleagues suggest meeting together to see how they might coordinate plans and materials across the curriculum. Ideas and possibilities are exchanged – and all of this without one instruction or suggestion from the school's management. For a short while, albeit in a temporary way, teachers genuinely take control of the curriculum. The fact that it involves extra work and effort is irrelevant; this is what education should be about and it's worth it. What is more, over the next couple of years such breaks from routine become regular events in the school.

Two years later, in my role as teacher educator, I take a group of beginning teachers to see – and participate in – the school's climate-change project, where the entire curriculum has been suspended for two weeks, with every lesson and every activity dedicated to discussion, production of art and writing, drama and media events about this central topic. The event is a great success and at the end of it, as I work with the school on an evaluation, it has been almost universally acclaimed. An experienced teacher tells me rather poignantly that 'these two weeks have reminded me of why I became a teacher some twenty years ago. It's also made me ashamed of what I have allowed myself to become.' A student teacher comments that 'it made me see that the utopian ideas I am mustering at the moment actually work!' (Berry, 2009: 35). At this point, it is worth reiterating one of the central ideas of this book: the idea that the GERM and everything associated with it has completely killed off the spirit and enthusiasm of teachers is mistaken. That is not to underestimate the difficulty of swimming against this particular tide, but such episodes – and they are far from isolated events in schools – give the lie to the idea that the modern teacher is the automaton deliverer of someone else's goods. Sometimes all it takes is a brave soul to speak up at a staff meeting and take a punt – it may be the day when he or she hits the right note – to get support from colleagues.

Such episodes of creativity don't, by their very nature, fit neatly into measurable and recordable systems. A nervousness persists among school leaders, many of whom will privately acknowledge that, like the beginning teacher, this approach is what they came into teaching for. Nevertheless, they fret about whether it will translate into 'good results'. Such anxiety stems from an incomplete appreciation of how children learn. The great pedagogical thinkers – Vygotsky, Piaget, Bruner, Freire – whose work has been stripped out of training and professional development, would have been able to tell them to relax. Learning does not take place incrementally and in a sequential way, as inconvenient as this may be for institutional organizations. I am always entertained by a standard Ofsted-type question used in observations and on learning walks: 'how do you know what they learnt in that lesson?' Quite how anyone could confidently answer such a question is beyond my comprehension. What was 'learnt' could well be forgotten by the start of the next lesson: conversely, a key point may be remembered on the walk home or simply when lounging in front of the TV.

Obsessed as we have become by measurability, we have lost sight of what we know about pedagogy. But to illustrate that teachers can see beyond this narrow agenda, I turn to the second, current episode of potential resistance.

Entirely independently of previous communication, I hear that teachers in Grace School are working as part of a Facebook campaign entitled 'You can't test this'. Intrigued, I log on to have a look. I hope it will be in full flow by the time this book is published. The basic premise is clear: as a reaction to the idea that for something to be worthwhile it has to be measurable, teachers in primary schools are looking to engage their children in learning in ways that are neither linear nor restricted. Education and learning remain firmly at the centre of what they wish to achieve, it's that they wish to achieve it by embarking on journeys that are scenic rather than functional. A primary school teacher on Facebook captures the spirit of the project thus:

> I have asked my lovely inventive class what could be learnt under this heading (i.e. the 'untestable'): a drumming pattern, a piece of anime art, a rap poem, a karate kata exercise, counting to ten in different languages, a skipping song and how to play elastics were suggested, amongst others ideas.

Other contributions exude inventiveness, fun and, above all, learning. In various suggestions to colleagues, teachers ask them to get their class to imagine a world without right-angles; they encourage children to spend some time actually going out and being hunter-gatherers (the mind does boggle a little here!) or to build an igloo out of recycled plastic milk cartons. Links are provided to articles and books teachers may find useful and inspiring and there is constant encouragement to 'carry on teaching brilliant things that are being squeezed from the curriculum'. Meetings are set up where teachers can meet and talk about such projects and plans. Such energy and commitment defies the idea that this is a profession so downtrodden that it has slipped into dull conformity. Nonetheless, the point bears restating: this commitment to children and their learning goes on *despite* the obstacles placed in teachers' way by governments and school leaderships who have been dragged, however reluctantly, into fighting for their market share. Resistance to the GERM, as shown in these examples, comes from teachers themselves taking responsibility for their profession and refusing to wait for the permission of experts and authorities.

The existence of 'You can't test this' on Facebook is significant because it is through social media that the voice of the teacher can now operate with great impact. In recent years the *Guardian* newspaper's *Secret*

Teacher has established a loyal and enthusiastic following as the column exposes some of the idiocies of modern marketized education and its consequences for young people and their teachers alike. Jane Manzone's brilliantly lively *@Hey Miss Smith* and Debra Kidd's blog have similarly found a way of speaking to *and* for teachers – the latter being a skill that has consistently eluded government departments. I arrange to speak to one of the most prolific of education tweeters, Emma Ann Hardy, whose advocacy and great skill in this medium is now widely recognized and admired (see Hardy, 2014).

   I begin by asking her how, in such demanding times, a primary school teacher finds the time and energy to maintain her social media profile. In her reply it is apparent that it is her commitment to the idea of a teaching community that energizes her. Correspondent to earlier comments in this book about the lack of real and metaphorical space for the interchange of ideas, she reinforces observations in her article (Hardy, 2014: 266) that 'discussions on pedagogy are constrained by the motivations of whoever it is who sets the agenda and their position within the school' and that it needs 'a brave teacher to initiate a discussion on pedagogy within the confines of a staff meeting'. She recognizes the understandable timidity of her colleagues who, like those wary of the learning walker, feel it sensible to keep their reservations to themselves. Hardy tells me that:

> There are still many teachers though that will contact me privately to say they agree with me but for various reasons they don't feel able to do so publicly. Teachers working in classrooms across the country know from their own day-to-day experience that the changes are increasing stress for children. The curriculum diet has been narrowed and the testing culture has not improved standards and instead only improved the ability to sit tests.

Social media and digital communications have the function of giving space to such teachers but, in the wider perspective, what this continues to show is a profession that still holds firmly to the notion of 'something better'. In Hardy's view social media platforms allow the sharing of ideas amongst a community that has 'always been hungry to develop' but which has been constrained by 'being unable to have meaningful and detailed debates during working hours'. She recognizes that social media are not a panacea: there are attendant dangers of homogeneity of thought and a new set of orthodoxies could become entrenched in the virtual world. But, she remains adamant that this tool, created by teachers for teachers, must be cherished and developed.

If more traditional readers are tempted into thinking that relationships forged in cyberspace may not be effective in taking the profession forward, they would be forced to think again. In an enterprise that has the old organizing hands of trade unions and teacher associations looking on enviously, Hardy and Debra Kidd galvanized the online community at a conference in 2014 in Leeds. Advertised only through social media, *Northern Rocks* attracted 500 teachers and was sold out seven months in advance. The introduction to its website report captures the excitement, vitality and, above all, the agency of the event:

> The first Northern Rocks Education Conference #Nrocks was held on Saturday 7th June 2014 at Leeds Metropolitan University. 500 teachers gathered in the rain to reclaim their profession. And we liked it, so we will do it again next year. We are teachers who thought that a major teaching and learning event in the North of England was long overdue. We are teachers who thought it was time to self organise and share best practice. We had a fabulous day, populated by people passionate about education who donated their time for free because they care.
>
> (northernrocks2014.wordpress.com)

Not an ambitious headteacher after an award, not a consultant, not an inspector and not an expert in sight – other than the clear classroom expertise brought to the event by teachers themselves. Sahlberg talks of how the GERM is characterized by low-risk ways of achieving teaching goals. Hardy tells me about how this conference and the ambitions of those who attended it have flown in the face of such an approach. Reiterating her observation about a prevailing hunger for ideas, she tells me that 'social media has also opened up the political debate by making it more accessible – and teachers have opinions they want to share too'. In an idea that resonates with the basic thesis of this book, she talks of how optimism, rather than weary acceptance of the GERM (a term she uses readily) is one characteristic of those attending the conference. 'What we wanted was an event that left attendees feeling good about being teachers, with a variety of ideas to take away and greater knowledge of the ideas that are shaping education'. In both the world of teachers using social media and in the more traditional arena of meeting face-to-face, the spirit of these teachers is far from crushed.

This important idea that teachers have the capacity to change things for themselves without waiting for permission from a higher authority is central to the work of writer and campaigner Terry Wrigley. In *Changing Schools* (Wrigley *et al.*, 2012) he and his co-authors look at projects and educational enterprises around the world where groups of teachers, parents and others in that community have established educational settings based on sound pedagogical principles, not on the transient requirements of any particular government and authority. Many of these projects are also characterized by a commitment to social justice and equality of opportunity. Central to all these examples is a firm belief that teachers should not be and are not content with relying on the dubious evidence and research of those driven by neoliberal agendas. Ironically, however, such challenge can even end up fitting that bill as well. When he describes how a concerted and cooperative approach resulted in the improvement of an English primary school deemed to be failing, Wrigley draws an interesting conclusion:

> With research ... staff can make their classrooms and schools sites of inquiry, connecting their work to government policy agendas and *critical readings* of school effectiveness and school improvement. They produce many credible findings which consider conclusions and recommendations for policy and practice.
>
> (Wrigley *et al.*, 2012: 147 – my emphases)

In common with this book, the authors share the purpose, so deftly expressed by the critic Raymond Williams, of making hope practical rather than despair convincing. Part of this hope must lie in the placing of rigorous research, genuine reflection and the sharing of ideas in the hands of teachers themselves.

Perhaps the overriding frustration for those thousands of teachers who know that the GERM has such a deleterious effect on teaching and learning is that, in the final analysis, its principal demands just aren't necessary. I've made the point several times but it bears repeating: no one – but no one – is suggesting that young people shouldn't achieve exam and test success and no one in their right mind would wish to harm the life-chances of young people. But the pursuit of these outcomes at the expense of a wider and more critical engagement with pedagogy and learning is not necessary or sensible. What is more, it diminishes the educational experience for teachers and students alike. Headteacher Alison Peacock, who has the ear of the great and the good and who has been recognized for her achievements in her role as an educational leader, captures this perfectly in her writings and actions. Writing of her leadership of the *Learning Without Limits* project (learningwithoutlimits.educ.cam.uk) she explains that:

> Politicians would have us believe that parents value scores and levels above everything else. Our experience has been the opposite. We find that what our parents really want to know is whether their children are understood, valued and inspired. They want to know that their children are happy and resilient, that they love learning and are making progress.
>
> (Peacock, 2012)

In her explanation of how she turned a school in difficult circumstances into one that not only became highly rated by Ofsted, but which also dismantled the limits that characterize so much of what has happened in schools over the last quarter of a century, she recounts how teachers helped to shape classroom activity to transform children's ability to learn. Children themselves were active agents in the development of their learning capacity as the school became an authentic learning community committed to fostering the potential of the pupils. The genuine involvement of a wider community of governors and parents and other local authority – i.e. non-privatized – schools was also central to the project. Peacock and her colleagues show how they have seen through the confidence trick, played on teachers by successive governments, which would have us believe that parents see their children's progress purely in terms of test outcomes:

> At parents' evenings, parents find themselves hearing about their children's learning not in all its rich and multifaceted variety, but about their levels. Their child they may be bewildered to be told, 'is a secure 3b in reading' but 'only a 2c in writing'. Teachers are encouraged to plan, predict report on progress and express concerns specifically in terms of levels.
>
> (Swann *et al.*, 2012: 19)

The alternative that has been built is a community of learners bound together by a principled pedagogic model established through trust and dialogue – and not through the adherence to the reductive model of government diktats. It is critical to understand that this is not some evangelical experiment built on a leap of faith: this is an approach to education, echoing as it does the instincts of many teachers, created through an understanding of pedagogic principles and, above all, of how people learn.

A final comment on the obsession with levels and scores to which these authors refer and which has dominated so much of the discourse in schools in recent years: The fact is that it is no longer a requirement to use them, but like the long-term prisoner disorientated and paralysed by the reality of freedom, many schools are finding it difficult to break free from their entrapment and persist with using them for internal audit and scrutiny. Similarly, despite unequivocal comment from Ofsted to schools to stop constantly reviewing learning in individual lessons, to reduce the shuffling from one activity to another and to stop producing over-detailed lesson plans (Ofsted, 2013), many of these imagined requirements dominate the practice of many school leaders and managers. We shouldn't be surprised by this. GERM-ridden practices have become firmly established and a central feature of this is the use of corporate management techniques driven by test-based accountability policies. Such regimes may not disappear overnight – but it is clear that there are plenty of teachers and school leaders out there who are ready and able to challenge them.

This chapter has looked at ways in which undefeated teachers can take matters into their own hands. We move on to conclude that, as encouraging as the challenge by teachers to the GERM is, it is only by placing this potential resistance firmly within a broader context that we can hope to bring about sustainable change.

Chapter 9

Undefeated – but how do we become GERM free?

On Karl Marx's gravestone is inscribed the famous epigram: 'The philosophers have only interpreted the world. The point, however, is to change it.' Readers could be excused if they were to question quite how relevant the old boy might still be in the connected, networked, post-modern world of the contemporary teacher and student. This chapter offers a sober appraisal of how the undefeated voice of the committed teacher might help to change the world – and become the prominent voice in the clamour of the market place. I place teachers, their schools and their managers firmly in the societal, political and economic circumstances of England today. To say that these circumstances characterize a society that is fragile and uncertain is a major understatement. At the time of writing, Europe's political leaders are agonizing over ways to deal with refugees whose plight derives from the very actions of those politicians; a housing crisis is enveloping parts of England as the acquisition of property as an investment commodity becomes ever more prevalent, and a publicly owned bank is being sold off to private investors at a knock-down rate. Schools, teachers, parents and students do not live in a vacuum. One thing about which Marx was quite sure is that what we think and how we act are expressions of wider influences: it was not, he argued, the consciousness of men that determines their being but, on the contrary, their social being that determines their consciousness. Not everyone believes this and it is not the purpose of this volume to enter into discussion about the merits of the argument. Nonetheless, what follows is underpinned by a firm proposition: teachers can beat the GERM, but to do so they will need to look beyond the school, its gates and even their own profession.

Notwithstanding my argument that teachers' resistance can only be successful as part of a far-reaching challenge to marketization and neoliberalism, it is with teachers and their organizations that we start. I reiterate a point made elsewhere; there was never a golden age of teacher autonomy and nor was there one of teacher militancy. It is, however, worth highlighting an episode in 1993 to demonstrate what is possible in terms of industrial action when allied to teachers' professional confidence.

The Education Reform Act (ERA) of 1988 introduced the National Curriculum. Although this was the most immediate effect of the legislation for teachers, its other provisions, which opened the way for schools to become independent financial units unbridled by local authority control, were just as far-reaching. As schools found themselves placed in the invidious situation of 'competing' with their neighbours for pupils, the possibility of league tables – considered too risible for sensible contemplation when first mooted – became a reality. For the compilation of league tables, results were needed. For measurable results, standardized tests were the quickest and easiest means of achieving these. The GERM had begun its period of incubation. The first standardized tests (SATS) in English, maths, science and technology – which was eventually dropped as a 'core' subject later in the decade as the feasibility of testing too many subjects became clear even to the most bull-headed of the testing advocates – were to take place in the Spring of 1993. Teachers, understanding the threat to their professional autonomy and the well-being of their students, refused to comply.

I emphasize the point that teachers were prepared to take industrial action – the percentages voting to do so were overwhelming with a turnout of over 90 per cent – not in order to demand improvements in pay or conditions but to defend the content of the curriculum and their professional autonomy (Coles, 1994; Jones, 1994). This testament to teachers' professional confidence is extraordinary and there has been no such manifestation of professional confidence on the part of teachers in the UK since (Berry, 2009). Again, it is important not to overstate the case: eventually, the Conservative government of the day manoeuvred matters so that the tests were established and their Labour successors proved themselves to be just as committed to them. None of this prevented the continuation of the campaign and the eventual scrapping of tests for 14-year-olds some dozen years later. The strength and brief success of this opposition stemmed from teachers' willingness to court parental support for their actions which, in one local campaign after another, was clear. In one of the most recent instances of teacher militancy in an international context, this garnering of wider support for teachers' actions has also been central to its impact.

In 2012, teachers in Chicago went on all-out strike for nine days in a chapter of resistance that was their first major industrial action for 25 years. The concerns of these teachers and their union, the Chicago Teachers Union (CTU), all stemmed from the marketization of the school system, cuts in provision – particularly for more vulnerable students and their families – and the increasing use of student test scores to determine the pay and tenure of teachers. In common with those teachers and public servants everywhere who eventually decide that the withholding of their labour is the only persuasive weapon left to them, the CTU knew that it would face the opprobrium of hostile politicians and media – especially against populist arguments about such industrial action being deemed archaic and harmful to students. Activists within the CTU were alert to such accusations and ensured that from the start of their campaign they kept in close contact with parents, community groups and other sets of workers who faced similar threats from privatization and marketization:

> The consensus in Chicago and around the country seemed to be that teachers' unions very existence was hated by most; going on strike was not even an option, since doing so would only further widen the gap between the public and the unions. But the CTU had managed to convince the public that the strike was not reflective of selfishness – it was the very means by which the union would accomplish a progressive education agenda. Neoliberal forces had long attempted to turn average people against public sector unions' struggles by framing any public workers' demands as coming at individual taxpayer's expense; in Chicago, that attempt failed.
>
> (Uetricht, 2014: 71)

In the same way that their counterparts in England had campaigned successfully by demonstrating that the impact of the market was deleterious to the welfare of students and the education system in general, so the Chicago teachers made some gains through their efforts. To believe that either the SATs campaign in England in 1993 or the CTU strike of 2012 were unqualified success stories is disingenuous. What both prove, however, is that by forming wider alliances, the possibilities for resistance are opened up.

More recently in England, alliances of this sort have sprung up throughout the country as parents campaign with teachers to prevent schools becoming academies. In conversation with Alasdair Smith, the tireless organizer of the Anti Academies Alliance (*www.antiacademies.org.uk*), he tells me about the campaigning efforts amongst parents and communities he has encountered. There is an understanding that their concerns go beyond the understandable ones of protecting their own children's schools to the issue of protecting public service from becoming private enterprise. 'The GERM has got hegemony but not approval,' he suggests, 'and there is a definite willingness to campaign.' The weight of the Education and Adoption Bill (Parliament 2015a) has made it more difficult for such campaigns to be sustained and Smith finds this doubly frustrating because of lack of evidence of the effectiveness of academy conversion.

He is right to be sceptical. Chaired by a member of the Conservative party, the Education Committee of the House of Commons draws the conclusion that 'academization is not always successful nor is it the only proven alternative for a struggling school' (Parliament 2015b: 4). Such unequivocal comment gives credence to Smith's assessment that there is 'no statistical proof that academies work. The push to conversion is ideological, not academic.' However, even though parents and teachers continue to demonstrate readiness to voice opposition to governments determined to push through this aspect of the neoliberal agenda, can such movements alone overcome the worst effects of the GERM? Our conversation turns to the possibility of opening a broader, national campaign for education that can win the support of teachers, parents and workers for a system that is not led by the need to produce, reduce, quantify and stratify.

On the face of it, this should be easy. If, as the old saying goes, the devil has all the best tunes, then it is the educators who must be the devil. In terms of educational research, much of what has been undertaken for the past 25 years has challenged the notion that evidence-based enquiry into how to produce better results is the only viable form of such research. It may well be the only form those in power will wish to acknowledge, but it reduces such research to little more than a quest for producing the best test results, irrespective of what such a process means for the broader education of students and society. An experience of mine illustrates this perfectly.

It is September 2010 and I am sitting in plush surroundings at the Department for Business, Innovation and Skills. I am at an event entitled 'A development day for education researchers in the UK'. Note that I am not at the Department for Education (DfE) – but that's another story: educational research and business are now, apparently, comfortable bedfellows. The event was originally scheduled for late April of that year, by the education department's predecessor, the Department for Children, Schools and Families, but the meeting has been postponed until after the May election. By this time, both the title of the event and its purpose have been altered. Originally proposed as a 'development day for education researchers *working in universities*' (my emphases), it has become a 'development day for education researchers in the UK'. The purpose of the original conference was to help researchers improve 'the reach of your research and opportunities for impact of research on policy and practice'. This has become reduced to 'supporting better use of research by practitioners and policy staff'. The drastic shift in this revised intention becomes clearer as the conference progresses.

A senior social researcher at the DfE expresses the unequivocal view that qualitative data will not be welcome, alerting those present to the requirement to produce quantitative data that clearly identifies an impact on standards. The Deputy Director of 14–19 education is equally clear: research that challenges or interrogates the current ideological position is unlikely to be treated with any seriousness. David Silverman, whose work is a must for any educational researcher, observes that 'governments favour quantitative research because it mimics the research of its own agencies' (Silverman, 2006: 35). And listening to these senior mandarins, it is impossible to argue with that proposition. Bring us research that improves test results or don't bother calling.

To reiterate a point made earlier: no teacher wants to depress students' grades, and a good deal of effort goes into producing the best outcomes that can work to their advantage. That, however, is not the same as only validating research concerned solely with the narrow and reductive business of the generation of such grades. And this presents the researchers, those with the best tunes, with a problem. Put baldly, if you want to embark on educational research that goes beyond the academic community and into the corridors of power, you had better do the sort of research that those who preside there want you to do. If not, funding won't be forthcoming and your work will be unwelcome. In a neoliberal world, where the 'outputs' of academics are subject to measurability and scrutiny through the Research Excellence Framework (REF), which has profound implications for tenure and promotion, this almost amounts to a 'comply or perish' situation for researchers. Writing in 2008, educational researcher Martin Hammersley warned fellow researchers that to tail-end government agendas was almost tantamount to collusion. 'Attempts to render educational research accountable parallel the reforms that have been carried out within the school system. What has happened there … is a deprofessionalization of teachers' (Hammersley, 2008: 759). He returns to the theme in 2013, bringing into question the entire notion that the effectiveness of social practice can be captured in figures and data (Hammersley, 2013). The opening of a wider debate about education, which challenges the current hegemonic notion that all that matters is raw results, becomes even more challenging if the people in power wilfully choose to ignore those whose research contradicts what they wish to hear.

Despite the fact that the voices of non-compliant academics have to struggle to make an impact on the powerful, teachers themselves remain fully prepared to sustain a dialogue about what education should be for, which transcends the demands of the GERM. The exploration of the proliferation of discussion by teachers about pedagogical matters through social media, described in the last chapter, evidences this willingness on their part. The excellent Reclaiming Schools website and blog (*www.reclaimingschools. org*), with its invitation to debate five central principles of accountability, curriculum and assessment, school governance, social justice and teacher professionalism, attracts contributions and comment of the highest order from teachers. It is true that this sort of commentary from teachers and those who research into their practice is often treated with disdain and suspicion by the people in power. Such a response is deeply disappointing. One might wish that those charged with organizing and funding the education of the nation's children would welcome the informed engagement of those who carry out the daily work that makes this happen. Dissent, even debate, it appears, equates to heresy when the market holds sway – but teachers still insist on thinking, speaking and writing about their practice in ways that defy what governments want.

Up to this point in our discussion of how the undefeated voice of the teacher can make itself heard, we have considered how teachers' actions, with the backing of a wider community, may provide an opportunity for this to happen. This, in its turn, presents possibilities of opening up a broader debate about the nature and purpose of education. We have seen how teachers are willing to establish their own platforms to investigate and interrogate their practice. The book has highlighted the ways that, given the opportunity to do so, teachers refuse to abandon their own concepts of what authentic and meaningful teaching and learning look like.

How, then, to change things? The basic argument here remains the same: any discussion about education in a neoliberal age needs to take place with a clear understanding that the way in which this particular social practice is arranged is itself a function of the dominant ideology of that age. To challenge what takes place in schools requires that we do not see this in isolation but rather as a manifestation of wider forces. To illustrate this, we go back to where we started the book: Finland and the work of Pasi Sahlberg.

But first, an obvious caveat. Finland is not a model society. It has high rates of alcoholism, murder and suicide (World Health Organization, 2013) – and it's horribly dark for much of the year. A quick scan through various news sources shows it to be as subject as any developed nation to pressures related to social injustice and financial insecurity. In conversation with Sahlberg, *Washington Post* journalist Valerie Strauss asks why other developed nations don't just appropriate Finland's successful educational methods and apply them in their own country (Strauss, 2012). Sahlberg's answer is instructive. He begins by pointing out that school funding in Finland is based entirely on a formula guaranteeing equal allocation of resources, regardless of location or the wealth of communities. Schools are autonomous and teachers' professionalism trusted. Teaching itself is a highly desirable profession, requiring a research-based master's degree; applicants far outnumber available places and have done so for years. The education system, Sahlberg points out, is interwoven in the surrounding welfare state and, above all, whereas 'in the United States , education is mostly viewed as a private effort leading to individual good … in Finland, education is viewed primarily as a public effort serving a public purpose'.

The implication here is clear: if we wish to promote a different notion of what we believe teaching and learning should be, we need to espouse a different view of what they are for. Any 'national debate' needs to start from here, not from a narrow conversation about how we increase the number of Level 4s or GCSE A–Cs. As my Latin teachers might have intoned, *post hoc ergo propter hoc*; don't assume a sequence of events to be 'cause and effect' and, in the case of educating our children, don't believe that you can lift practices from one environment and make them effective in another. This is important because the idea of 'policy tourism' is influential with politicians looking for a quick fix. Maths results are better in Singapore, so let's teach maths like them: Chinese schools produce great science results, let's do it the Chinese way. Such examples regularly crop up in politicians' discourse (DfE, 2014b) – conveniently overlooking the fact that these are different societies from England's in a whole range of ways. What happens in schools cannot be seen in isolation from what happens in the political, economic and societal conditions in which that school exists.

If, therefore, opening any debate about the nature of the education means challenging some of the fundamentals of how society is organized, is this feasible? Is it not the case that schools, howsoever liberal they would like to think themselves, are now so entrenched in the business of producing outcomes that any discussion of alternative practice becomes a fanciful luxury? And aren't parents themselves now educated into demanding outcomes? And students too? Is it just wishful thinking to imagine that new social movements that challenge the very basis of how schools currently work – and for what purpose – could emerge? Could teachers, notwithstanding their enduring adherence to a liberal humanist idea of education, be part of such a movement at the same time that scrutiny, observation and measurability ensure that they toe the line and are able to pay their bills?

At this point I would love to be able to deliver the silver bullet and proclaim that such organized resistance, delivered as part of a wholesale change in how society views what education is for, is an iron certainty. That promise cannot be given. However, I finish the book by thinking about possibilities of such resistance – ways in which this undefeated voice can eliminate the GERM.

It is the critic Fredric Jameson to whom the observation is usually attributed, that it is easier for most people to envisage the end of the world than the end of capitalism. I am not arguing here that a change to the way we perceive education is conditional on the overthrow of capitalism (although that could help), but that in a febrile, uncertain global situation – and the GERM itself exists as a function of globalization – possibilities for change present themselves in unpredictable ways and sometimes take place with great rapidity. I offer three observations as examples.

First, in 2011 eminent academic and critic Terry Eagleton published a book entitled *Why Marx Was Right* (Eagleton, 2011). In the wake of the 2008 financial crash, as people sought explanations for the demise of the apparently impregnable fortress of international finance, there was an upsurge in the sales of Marx's work (Connolly, 2008). What was once considered archaic and beyond sensible consideration was now seen by some as something that could potentially cast light on a calamitous situation. Marx became fashionable and, more importantly, was taken seriously. Again, I am not advocating Marxism as the way forward to achieve teacher autonomy and better learning for young people. The point of interest is that when material conditions alter, so do people's ideas. As Eagleton (2011: xi) pithily suggests when explaining the revival of the term in general discourse, 'you can tell that the capitalist system is in trouble when people start talking about capitalism'. Equally, Eagleton might have observed that such changes are just as recognizable when an internationally renowned academic publishes a work defending Marx under the auspices of an Ivy League university. No social system lasts forever.

Second, and as a development of this idea, another eminent commentator, Noam Chomsky, observes that addressing inequality on a global scale 'is now almost a standard framework of discussion … (which) exposes the heartlessness and inhumanity of the system' and which produces a response that 'offers meaningful solidarity to those being crushed by it' (Chomsky, 2012: 13). Chomsky points to social movements and their actions across parts of the globe, including in the belly of the beast in the

United States, which belie notions that individualism holds sway and that solidarity, especially among the young, the networked and the savvy, is a thing of the past. He points out that those who choose to occupy and demonstrate are often those who should, on the face of it, be enjoying the economic and social benefits of advanced and mature democracies. That they choose to act side by side with the disadvantaged is an expression of the growing international solidarity of which he speaks.

Finally, journalist and broadcaster Paul Mason explores this growth of solidarity and this 'standard framework' of addressing inequality in his observations of protest around the world (Mason, 2012). He challenges the notion that a generation welded to smartphones, chasing brand names and unable to form social relationships other than online has become completely disconnected from political issues. His examples are global, but his commentary on the student protest in London in 2010 – the first for well over 20 years – is local and illuminating. The protesters are not shabby; they deliver no leaflets; they do not stand on corners selling newspapers. He describes a fashionably dressed, elegant young woman making her way to an organizing meeting.

> Had she heard of the Polish trade union Solidarity? Shakes her head. Nothing at all ... I had no politics. I still don't subscribe to any. I'd probably say I was quite far left now – although I am not radical. I don't read newspapers.
>
> (Mason, 2012: 42)

None of this is to imply that, to paraphrase Mason, those out of the pages of trendy fashion magazines are forging a new revolutionary movement. As he points out:

> From Millbank (where students confronted police) to the summer riots, the scale of British discontent looks small beside the Arab Spring. But it was significant both sociologically and politically. Not only did it demonstrate the almost total disconnect between official politics and large sections of young people; it was also the moment that protest methods once known to a committed few were adopted by the uncommitted masses.
>
> (Mason, 2012: 62)

But what this does suggest is that, to borrow from Mark Twain, rumours of the death of the possibilities for social change are somewhat exaggerated. Protest, discontent and discourse addressing inequality have never

86

disappeared – and it is with some trepidation that I offer a final thought about the stubborn resilience of such thinking.

My trepidation stems from the fact that events may well have moved in peculiar ways between the writing, publication and the reading of this book – and so I hope that readers will understand the following example for what it is intended to be: a case of how things move in wildly unpredictable ways in a volatile political and economic global climate. I am writing this chapter in the autumn of 2015 and Jeremy Corbyn, a veteran politician with enduring left-leaning principles, has been elected as leader of Britain's Labour Party. Some twelve weeks earlier, bookmakers – who consistently remain better predictors of political trends than pollsters (Dolan and Falush, 2015) – were offering outlandish odds against the possibility of such an outcome. Promoting policies deemed by mainstream politicians to be outdated, unworkable and utopian, Corbyn gathered unprecedented public support from those who gladly embraced an agenda of equality, anti-privatization and fairness. This may be a short-lived phenomenon, but it fits with Chomsky's notion of the standard framework of discussion that exists to combat global inequality. Social and political movements in Greece and Spain are a further manifestation of unwillingness, particularly among the young, to accept that things always have to be the way they are.

To end this book, I reiterate its basic thesis: there are plenty of reasons to be cheerful. It is true that the globalized, marketized world of neoliberal education works relentlessly to make education a commodity and a private good. Governments and corporations strive to make or save money and then to demonstrate that any expenditure is good value. The model of education as means of producing human capital informs the actions of all these interested parties. They dutifully repeat mantras about 'all our children' and 'closing gaps'. I do not wish to suggest that as human beings all such proponents of the market are dreadful monsters. I have met many senior figures in education – heads, senior civil servants, even Ofsted inspectors – who will quietly admit that they don't quite know how they got involved in the mucky game of running education as a business. Yet at the end of this production line we have children in England tested more than their international counterparts, schools that run permanently in fear of inspection, and an enduring fractiousness about the production of meaningless data.

But tens of thousands of teachers don't buy this vision. They retain spirit, authenticity and vitality. Their principal problem is that they often have to smuggle these qualities into their lessons lest the watchful eye of the dull scrutineer misunderstands – and misreports – their actions. This final chapter has explored another challenge for teachers: how to coordinate their actions, act in unified resistance – preferably with parents, other workers and social movements (some of which may be forming as I write) – to ensure that their voice becomes hegemonic, the one that gets the societal echo it merits and the one that becomes the new 'common sense'.

I give the last words to two teachers. First to Danielle, a secondary teacher with ten years' experience, interviewed as part of the original study in 2010 and subsequently a regular correspondent with me on matters pertinent to teacher autonomy and children's independent learning. Danielle tells me how impatient she is with the need to measure, record and validate every last classroom action, thus echoing the thoughts and feelings of dozens of my respondents:

> If you're teaching lessons that genuinely have a purpose, that genuinely aim to get the kids somewhere by the end of it, whether it's a learning intention or objective or outcome or whatever you want to label it, and if it's pacey and engaging and fun really, if they're into it, all of those things you're nagged about will follow, and all of those things will naturally be in there.

Finally to Stephanie (her real name), a beginning teacher and the one chosen by her peers and lecturers to give the students' address at her graduation ceremony in 2015. Stephanie finishes with these words:

> Now I look forward, in anticipation, to meeting my class. To the child who has to have the last word, the child who can't sit still, the one who needs to be challenged, the one who says they have understood but hasn't got a clue what you just said, the child who daydreams, the child who is shy. I may not know them by name yet, but I soon will. Soon I will know how to get the best out of each and every one of them. I will never give up on any of them no matter how hard it gets. That's my job. My new profession.

I suggest that we leave Danielle and Stephanie to make their own decisions. Children will flourish in their hands.

References

Alexander, R. (2004) 'Still no pedagogy? Principle, pragmatism and compliance in primary education'. *Cambridge Journal of Education,* 34 (1), 7–33.

— (2010) 'Legacies, policies and prospects: One year on from the Cambridge Primary Review'. The Brian Simon Memorial Lecture. *Forum,* 53 (1), 71–92.

Apple, M. (2004) *Ideology and Curriculum.* London: Routledge.

Assessment and Qualifications Alliance (AQA) (2015) 'Explaining new GCSE grades'. Online. http://tinyurl.com/hyt2yh2 (accessed 12 September 2015).

Ball, S. (1999) 'Global trends in educational reform and the struggle for the soul of the teacher!' Paper presented at the British Educational Research Association Annual Conference, 2–5 September, 1999. Online. www.leeds.ac.uk/educol/documents/00001212.htm (accessed 15 May 2015).

— (2003) 'The teacher's soul and the terrors of performativity'. *Journal of Education Policy,* 18 (2), 215–228.

— (2008) *The Great Education Debate.* London: Policy Press.

Ball, S., and Olmedo, A. (2013) 'Care of the self, resistance and subjectivity under neoliberal governmentalism'. *Critical Studies in Education,* 54 (1), 85–96.

BBC (2010) 'Celebrations as last trapped Chile miner is rescued'. Online. www.bbc.co.uk/news/world-latin-america-11518015 (accessed 10 August 2015).

Benn, M. (2011) *School Wars: The battle for Britain's education.* London: Verso.

Bernstein, B. (1996) *Pedagogy, Symbolic Control and Identity: Theory, research, critique.* London: Taylor & Francis.

Berry, J. (2009) 'Can there be an alternative to the centralized curriculum in England?' *Improving Schools,* 12 (1), 33–41.

— (2013a) 'An investigation into teachers' professional autonomy in England: Implications for policy and practice'. PhD thesis. University of Hertfordshire.

— (2013b) 'Does Gove really want to set us free?' *Forum,* 54 (2), 273–284.

Bruner, J. (1960) *The Process of Education.* Cambridge, MA: Harvard University Press.

Burgess, S., Greaves, E., Vignoles, A., and Wilson, D. (2011) 'Parental choice of primary school in England: What types of school do different types of family really have available to them?' *Policy Studies,* 32 (5), 531–547.

Busher, H. (2006) *Understanding Educational Leadership: People, power and culture.* Buckingham: Open University Press.

Callaghan, J. (1976) Speech at Ruskin College. Online. www.theguardian.com/education/thegreatdebate/0,9857,564054,00.html (accessed 25 April 2015).

CBI (Confederation of British Industry) (2014) 'Gateway to growth'. Online. http://news.cbi.org.uk/business-issues/education-and-skills/gateway-to-growth-cbi-pearson-education-and-skills-survey-2015/

Chapman, C. (2002) 'Ofsted and school improvement: Teachers' perceptions of the inspection process in schools facing challenging circumstances'. *School Leadership and Management,* 22 (3), 257–272.

References

Children's Society (2015) 'The Good Childhood Report, 2015'. Online. www. childrenssociety.org.uk/sites/default/files/TheGoodChildhoodReport2015.pdf (accessed 22 August 2015).

Chitty, C. (2009) *Education Policy in Britain*. London: Palgrave Macmillan.

Chomsky, N. (2012) *Occupy*. London: Penguin.

Cole, G.D.H., and Postgate, R. (1938) *The Common People*. London: Methuen.

Coles, J. (1994) 'When enough was enough: The teachers' boycott of National Curriculum testing'. *Changing English*, 1 (2), 6–31.

Connolly, K. (2008) 'Booklovers turn to Karl Marx as financial crisis bites in Germany'. Online. www.theguardian.com/books/2008/oct/15/marx-germany-popularity-financial-crisis (accessed 7 September 2015).

Cox, B. (1995) *The Battle for the English Curriculum*. London: Hodder and Stoughton.

Dale, R. (1989) *The State and Education Policy*. Buckingham: Open University Press.

Davies, M., and Edwards, G. (1999) 'Will the curriculum caterpillar ever learn to fly?' *Cambridge Journal of Education*, 29 (2), 265–275.

Department for Education (DfE) (2011) 'Training our next generation of outstanding teachers'. Online. http://tinyurl.com/zyg2gwg (accessed 14 May 2015).

— (2014a) 'School Workforce in England: November 2013'. Online. http://tinyurl. com/nqxe6ww (accessed 2 July 2015).

— (2014b) 'Network of 32 maths hubs across England aims to raise standards'. Online. http://tinyurl.com/ll7h8qe (accessed 7 September 2015).

Department for Education and Skills (DfES) (2003) *Excellence and Enjoyment: A strategy for primary schools*. London: HMSO.

Didau, David (2013) 'So what is the point of INSET days?' Online. www. learningspy.co.uk/training/so-what-is-the-point-of-inset-days/ (accessed 1 October 2015).

Dolan, M. and Falush, S. (2015) 'Analysis: Bookies win again versus emotion-skewed opinion polls'. Reuters. Online. http://tinyurl.com/n7laqda (accessed 23 September 2015).

Eagleton, T. (2011) *Why Marx Was Right*. New Haven, CT: Yale University Press.

Fielding, M. (2001) 'Ofsted, inspection and betrayal of democracy'. *Journal of Philosophy of Education*, 35 (4), 695–704.

Firestone, W. (1993) 'Alternative arguments for generalizing from data as applied to qualitative research'. *Educational Researcher*, 22 (4), 16–23.

Freire, P. (1990) *Pedagogy of the Oppressed*. London: Penguin.

Friedman, M., and Friedman, R. (1980) *Free to Choose*. Harmondsworth: Penguin.

Gamble, A. (1988) *The Free Economy and the Strong State: The politics of Thatcherism*. Basingstoke: Macmillan.

Gillard, D. (2011) *Education in England: A brief history*. Online. www. educationengland.org.uk/history (accessed 14 May 2015).

Gove, M. (2013) 'I refuse to surrender to the Marxist teachers'. Online. http:// tinyurl.com/d4gq534 (accessed 14 May 2015).

Gramsci, A. (1971) *Selections from Prison Notebooks*. London: Lawrence and Wishart.

Gretton, J., and Jackson, M. (1976) *William Tyndale: Collapse of a school or a system?* London: Allen and Unwin.

Hammersley, M. (2008) 'Troubling criteria: A critical commentary on Furlong and Oancea's framework for assessing educational research'. *British Educational Research Journal,* 34 (6), 747–762.

— (2013) *The Myth of Research-based Policy and Practice.* London: Sage.

Hardy, E.A. (2014) 'Teachers are doing it for themselves: Using social media for professional development and advocacy'. *Forum,* 56 (2), 265–276.

Harris, S. (2007) *The Governance of Education: How neoliberalism is transforming policy and practice.* London: Continuum.

Harvey, D. (2005) *A Brief History of Neoliberalism.* Oxford: OUP.

Hayek, F. (1960) *The Constitution of Liberty.* London: Routledge Keegan Paul.

Holt, J. (1991) *How Children Learn.* Harmondsworth: Penguin.

Hutchings, M. (2015) *Exam Factories? The impact of accountability measures on children and young people.* National Union of Teachers. Online. www.teachers. org.uk/files/exam-factories.pdf (accessed 3 August 2015).

Jones, K. (1994) 'The teachers' boycotting of testing: A new kind of cultural politics'. *Changing English,* 2 (1), 84–110.

Jones, P.W. (2007) *World Bank Financing of Education.* London: Routledge.

Leavis, F.R. (1948) *The Great Tradition.* London: Chatto & Windus.

Lyotard, J.-F. (1984) *The Postmodern Condition: A report on knowledge.* Manchester: Manchester University Press.

Mansell, M. (2014) 'The strange case of the vanishing GCSE pupils'. *The Guardian.* Online. www.theguardian.com/education/2014/jan/21/gcse-pupils-disappearing-from-school-rolls (accessed 30 July 2015).

Mason, P. (2012) *Why it's Still Kicking Off Everywhere.* London: Verso.

Morgan, N. (2015) 'More academies, greater freedom'. Online. http://tinyurl.com/p9bdk5z (accessed 2 July 2015).

Morris, A., and Nash, M. (2013) *Pisa: Not just a league table.* Online. http://policyconsortium.co.uk/pisa-not-just-a-league-table/ (accessed 10 October 2015).

National College for Leadership of Schools and Children's Services (2010) *10 strong claims about successful school leadership.* Online. www.almaharris. co.uk/files/10strongclaims.pdf (accessed 24 August 2015).

National Union of Teachers (2015) 'Age discrimination in teaching'. Online. www. teachers.org.uk/node/23661 (accessed 29 July 2015).

OECD (2012) *Equity and Quality in Education: Supporting disadvantaged students and schools.* Online. http://dx.doi.org/10.1787/9789264130852-en (accessed 28 August 2015).

Ofsted (2013) *Moving English Forward.* Online. http://tinyurl.com/ja4pymk (accessed 28 August 2015).

Parliament (2012a) 'Annual Report of HM Chief Inspector, Ofsted'. Transcript of oral evidence taken before the Education Committee. Online. http://tinyurl.com/jsp57nq (accessed 29 July 2015).

— (2012b) *Great Teachers: Attracting, training and retaining the best.* Ch. 5: 'Retaining, valuing and developing teachers'. Online. http://tinyurl.com/d9tvktk (accessed 29 July 2015).

References

— (2015a) *Education and Adoption Bill*. Online. www.publications.parliament.uk/pa/bills/cbill/2015-2016/0004/16004.pdf (accessed 28 August 2015).

— (2015b) *Academies and Free Schools*. Online. www.publications.parliament.uk/pa/cm201415/cmselect/cmeduc/258/258.pdf (accessed 1 September 2015).

Peacock, A. (2012) 'Learning without limits'. Online. www.guardian.com/teacher-network/teacher-blog/2012/may/29/sats-abilty-learning-limits (accessed 10 October 2015).

Pearson (2013) 'Pearson 2012 Results'. Online. www.pearson.com/news/announcements/2013/february/pearson-2012-results.html (accessed 6 May 2015).

Robinson, S. (2012) 'Constructing teacher agency in response to the constraints of education policy: Adoption and adaptation'. *The Curriculum Journal*, 23 (2), 231–245.

Rosen, M. (2015) 'Dear Ms Morgan: Your guidance is a mini-syllabus on how to wreck poetry'. Online. http://tinyurl.com/onursvb (accessed 11 August 2015).

Sahlberg, P. (2012) *Finnish Lessons: What the world can learn from educational change in Finland*. New York: Teachers College Press.

Secretary of State for Education and Employment (1997) *Excellence in Schools*. London: HMSO. Online. www.educationengland.org.uk/documents/wp1997/excellence-in-schools.html (accessed 25 August 2015).

Selvarajah, S. (2015) 'Headhunters for headteachers: schools pay firms up to £50,000 to find leaders'. *The Guardian*. Online. http://tinyurl.com/p5m6hgm (accessed 24 August 2015).

Silverman, D. (2006) *Interpreting Qualitative Data*. London: Sage.

Simon, B. (1981) 'Why no pedagogy in England?' in Moon, B. and Shelton Mayes, A. (eds) (1994) *Teaching and Learning in the Secondary School*. London: Routledge.

Stewart, W. (2015) 'Leave research to the academics, John Hattie tells teachers'. Online. www.tes.com/news/school-news/breaking-news/leave-research-academics-john-hattie-tells-teachers (accessed 1 October 2015).

Strauss, V. (2012) *What the US can't learn from Finland about ed reform*. Online. http://tinyurl.com/dxqg2t4 (accessed 6 September 2015).

Swann, M., Peacock, A., Hart, S., and Drummond, M. (2012) *Creating Learning Without Limits*. Maidenhead: McGraw-Hill.

Uetricht, M. (2014) *Strike for America: Chicago teachers against austerity*. London: Verso.

Vygotsky, L.S. (1978) *Mind in Society: Development of higher psychological processes*. Cambridge, MA: Harvard.

Ward, H. (2015) 'Teacher training applications drop as recruitment crisis fears intensify'. *Times Educational Supplement*. Online. http://tinyurl.com/gldoatk (accessed 31 July 2015).

Wiliam, D. (2015) 'Why teaching will never be a research-based profession and why that's a Good Thing'. Online. www.dylanwiliam.org/Dylan_Wiliams_website/Presentations_files/2014-09-06%20ResearchED.pptx (accessed 1 October 2015).

Wilshaw, M. (2014) 'Check against delivery'. Speech to the North of England Education Conference, 15 January. Online. http://tinyurl.com/zxn7oaj (accessed 2 July 2015).

World Health Organization (2013) 'Finland'. Online. www.who.int/countries/fin/en/ (accessed 6 September 2015).

Wrigley, T., Thomson, P., and Lingard, B. (2012) *Changing Schools: Alternative ways to make a world of difference*. London: Routledge.

Index